DJ
Cookbook
Business Start-up Guide

Dan Titus

Foreword by
Dave Kreiner

Acknowledgements

Thanks to Jim Calkins who supported us with finance contributions. He has a way of explaining technical subjects that is easy to understand and comprehend. Thanks to Tony Crabtree for his contributions regarding equipment and sound. Special thanks to Dave Kreiner for his inspiration, which without this book would not have been written.

Publisher's Note

Printed in The United States of America
Published by Venture Marketing, Chino Hills, California, USA

Titus, Dan
The DJ Cookbook Business Start-up Guide
Includes references and index.
ISBN 1-58291-108-8

Design and illustration by Paul Daniels. Edited by Marilyn Weishaar.

Foreword

The DJ business has come a long way!

I started out as a musician about 15 years ago. A club I was working, called the Red Onion in Southern California, fired our band and hired me as a club DJ. I didn't have any DJ skills, but they were willing to teach me. With my band experience, ability to read a crowd, select music, and front man activities, I basically had an easy transition to live DJing. All I had to learn was how to push a buttons!

The DJ industry has evolved over the years mostly through technology. I remember the first CD players had 2 to 3 seconds of latency before the song actually started. It was near impossible to beat mix or slam with that long of a delay. The gear is just so much better now.

When I started DJing, I went to lots of clubs and borrowed ideas from the best club DJs. I wrote down their playlists, what they said, how they said it, and what they did with their mixes. If you are a mobile DJ, go to as many events as you can and study what is going on. Only then can you really know how to be the best you can be.

Today's mobile DJs, have to have music talent, performance skills, business experience and at the same time be an excellent salesman. If you don't have these skills, you can learn them. In the future salesmanship and a higher level of performance will be expected of all club and mobile DJs. Reading a crowd, extensive music knowledge, music programming skills, entertaining, and business skills will be vital to a DJs survival. The valuable business skills presented in *The DJ Cookbook: Business Start-up Guide*, will provide you the blueprints necessary to compete. Above all, remember, you *can* learn. Never quit!

Best of luck with your DJing and all your business endeavors!

Dave Kreiner
The Source DJ Supply

Never Quit.

Table of Contents

Introduction

Chapter 1: Preplanning

Contents

Chapter 3: Financial Planning

Chapter 4: Marketing

Contents

Chapter 6: Equipment

Contents

Introduction

You've got the talent.
Now get down to business!

Technology in recent years has brought about significant improvements in manufacturing techniques. Coupled with new smaller electronics and faster computer chips, prices for equipment have dropped dramatically. The clear-cut winner is the consumer and disc jockeys (DJs). More people have access to equipment. Therefore, more people are developing the necessary skills to become a DJ. Hence, people may have the desire to start a DJ service but have no idea how to begin.

This book is designed to help you start a DJ service. It is designed to acquaint you with concepts that you will need to form a new business. I have concentrated on the start-up aspects rather than the operational day-to-day aspects of running a service. For example, one of the key topics is how to develop your business plan. I have tried to include elements to address starting a DJ service from scratch.

This book has a Web site that accompanies it and is a key element for your success. It is assumed that you have basic DJ skills, computer skills, and that you can navigate your way around an IBM compatible system. This is important to get the most out of the Web site, and programs that go with this book.

How to Use This Book

This book is designed to be used as an action plan for starting your business. It is laid out in specific sections to attain this goal. Some of the chapters are grouped; others are specific to one particular topic. Therefore, you can skip around in this book rather than read it in a sequential manor.

Chapter 1: Preplanning

Chapter 1, *Preplanning,* is designed to expose you to a lot of information so that you will begin thinking about all the aspects that lie ahead. It asks many tough self-evaluation questions so that you will have a better understanding of your strengths and weaknesses. The chapter walks you through what will need to be accomplished in order to test the feasibility of your business idea. Explained are the different types of business entities, such as corporations and partnerships. The chapter basically acts as a large preplanning checklist that you can use to get started.

Chapters 2- 5: Business Plan Elements

Chapters 2 through 5 are grouped together. These are the chapters that explain what is needed to develop a detailed business plan and understand the financial information that will be required in the plan.

Chapter 2, *The Business Plan Primer*, will introduce you business plan basics. I will go go over the basic elements needed to create a business plan and explain the primary points that need to be covered in each section of the plan.

Chapter 3, *Financial Planning,* introduces key elements of finance and what you will need to know in order to add some of these elements to your business plan. Jim Calkin is my mentor in this area. Much of the information in this part of the book is excerpted from Jim's book, *Business Buyers Handbook.* The perspective in this chapter is for buying an existing business. However, the elements are the same for any business.

Chapter 4, *Marketing*, shows how to create a marketing plan. A marketing plan is a key element of your business plan, therefore, it is imperative that you have an understanding of the concepts presented in this chapter.

Chapter 5, *The Business Plan*, is a sample plan that you can study to see how all the elements fit together. It is laid out following the outline presented in Chapter 2.

Chapter 6: Equipment

Contributed by audio engineer and veteran live sound man, Tony Crabtree, this chapter outlines key concepts necessary for operating sound systems. From basic microphone concepts to proper gain structure, material presented here will guide you on your way to better shows.

Chapter 7: Operations

This chapter offers you basic practical tips for operating your DJ service. Included are sample forms and contracts that you can adopt for your business.

Chapter 8: Financing

This chapter provides an overview of some of the sources where you might find financing for your business. From partners, family, friends, government loan programs, to credit cards, this chapter offers strategies to help you get the necessary start-up capital.

Chapter 9: The Web Site

Here you will find an overview of the Web site that is designed to go along with this book. Look for the Web Connect logo, shown above, in the margins throughout this book. This will notify you about expanded chapter topics, books, or software that you can receive online. Simply fill out and return the registration form, which you will find in the back of this book, to qualify for this Web site access.

Appendix

In the appendix you will find reference material, such as bibliography and contact information.

Final Notes

Throughout this book I offer tips that are noted in the margins. Be sure to put your personal notes there too, as this will assist you with your critical thinking.

Again, in order to take full advantage of the software and spreadsheet templates that are at the Web site, and on the CD-ROM, it is assumed that you are able to use a computer, and the associated software for Internet access.

Finally, I hope that you find this book informative and I hope it helps you with your business endeavors.

Dan Titus

Preplanning

This chapter is designed to get you thinking about the many aspects of your new business and what you will need to accomplish from a tactical point. It is designed to test the feasibility of your business idea. From evaluating yourself as an individual to providing detailed checklists, it will help you with preplanning. There are many questions asked and you will need to know the answers before you move forward with your endeavors. Use this chapter as a tool to honestly assess yourself.

The U.S. Small Business Administration (SBA) has compiled a going-into-business checklist, which is designed to help you stay on track. The checklist asks questions that can help reveal fail points in your thinking. Fail points are areas that can have negative consequences once you launch your company. If you can answer these questions thoroughly and positively, you will be prepared to begin the quest of starting your own business. If you stumble on these questions, you may have some more studying to do.

Successful businesses begin with a practical plan. Entrepreneurs need a solid background in the businesses they choose to launch.

The SBA correctly identifies these qualities for a successful start-up:

- A practical business plan - Although not a quality, it is critical to your success.
- The dedication and willingness to sacrifice to reach your goal.
- Technical skills (If you launch a trucking company, you better know about trucking.)
- Knowledge of management, finance, bookkeeping, and market analysis.

Clarify your reasons for launching, and even more importantly identify your strengths and weaknesses. Once you've answered these questions, you'll have a good idea whether you should launch right away, or hold off for awhile.

Why Do You Want to Start Business?

As a first step, ask yourself why you want to start business. Identifying your reasons is important. People start a business for different reasons, including:

• Freedom from the daily work routine.
• Being your own boss.
• Doing what you want when you want to do it.
• Improving your standard of living.
• Freedom from a boring job.
• Having a product or service you believe will create a demand.

Some reasons are better than others. No reason is wrong; but be aware that there are tradeoffs. You can escape the daily routine of employment only to find that business ownership is more demanding.

The checklist asks the difficult questions that can reveal holes in your thinking, that may have dire consequences once you launch your company.

Self-Evaluation

Do You Have What it Takes?

Going into business requires particular personal characteristics. This portion of the checklist explores your personal attributes. It is important to stay objective, and above all, be honest about your capabilities.

The goal here is to access your strengths and weakness, so you can develop a strategy to deal with those aspects of your new business that you will be directly involved with, and those that you will delegate to other parties. You may be great at finance and you may have the computer aptitude to develop your own business promotion kit. However, you may not have the knowledge, or desire, to pursue all the marketing aspects of writing a business plan. Therefore, seek help in marketing.

Personal Characteristics

• Are you a leader? Do others turn to you for help in making decisions?
• Do you make decisions easily?
• Do you enjoy competition?
• Do you have the required self-discipline?
• Do you usually plan ahead? Impulse is a dangerous trait in business owners.
• Do you like to meet new people?
• Do you get along well with a wide range of people?
• Can you delay gratification?

Personal Conditions

This group of questions is vitally important for new business owners.

• Do you have the physical, emotional, and financial strength to launch a new company?
• Do you realize that running your own business may require working 12-16 hours a day, six days a week, even Sundays and holidays?
• Do you have the physical stamina to handle the workload and schedule?
• Do you have the emotional strength to withstand the strain of the disappointments and rejection that invariably come with launching a new enterprise?

Consequences of Launching a Business

• Are you prepared to possibly lower your standard of living until your business is firmly established? It can take time to regain your standard of living if you quit a high-paying job.
• Is your family prepared to go along with the strains they also must bear? Launching without the support of family can kill a business.
• Are you prepared to lose your savings? There's a reason they call it risk. Many people lose their entire investment.

You can escape the daily routine of employment only to find that business ownership is much more demanding.

Be ready to eat, drink, and sleep your new business. Like a newly planted plant, there will be a critical time while your business takes root.
Your time will be needed to develop systems that will help run the busi-

ness. At the same time, you more than likely will be running the day-to-day operations.

Your Business Knowledge

It is unlikely that you possess all of the particular skills and experience that are critical for business success. You'll need to learn as much as you can before starting your business.

• Have you ever worked in a managerial or supervisory capacity?
• Have you ever worked in a business similar to the one you want to start?
• Have you had any business classes in school?
• If you discover you don't have the basic skills needed for your business, will you be willing to delay your plans until you've acquired the necessary skills?

Feasibility

Your business ideas and your market feasibility will become basic elements of your business plan. See chapters 2 and 5 for details about business plans. For now you can make a preliminary outline based on the following criteria. Briefly answer the questions the best that you can. The objective here is to test the feasibility of your business idea.

Your Business Idea

Many entrepreneurs dive into business blinded by their dream before evaluating the potential of the business. Before you invest time, effort, and money, the following exercise will help you differentiate good ideas from those ideas destined to fail.

• Identify and briefly describe the business you plan to start.
• Identify the products or services you plan to sell.
• Does your product or service satisfy an unfilled need among potential customers you can reach?
• Can you make a profit? How long will it take to make a profit?
• Will your product or service be competitive based on quality, selection, price, or location?
• What will it cost to produce, advertise, sell & deliver?

The Market

To succeed, you need to know who your customers are. To learn about your market, you need to analyze it. You don't have to be an expert market analyst to learn about your marketplace, nor does the analysis have to be costly. Analyzing your market is a way to gather facts about potential customers and a way to determine the demand for your products or services. The more information you have, the greater your chances of capturing a profitable segment of the market.

Sometimes the best market information is simply the knowledge you have gathered by being an enthusiast for the market: If you launch a taco stand, a lifelong interest in tacos helps. You can approach this several ways, however, it is critical to learn your market before investing time and money in an enterprise.

These questions will help you gather the information necessary to analyze your market and determine if your products or services will sell.

- Who are your customers and how often will they purchase?
- Do you understand their needs and desires?
- Do you know where they live and how to reach them?
- Will you offer the kind of services that are missing from the market but are likely to be valued?
- Will your service prices be competitive in quality and value?
- Do you know how to promote your service to your target customers?
- Do you understand how your business concept compares with competitors'?

Many entrepreneurs go into business blinded by dreams, unable to thoroughly evaluate its potential.

Business Start-Up Planning

So far this checklist has helped you identify questions and problems you will face determining if your idea is feasible and converting your idea into reality. Through self-analysis you have learned your personal qualifications and deficiencies, and through market analysis you have learned if there is a demand for your service.

TIP
See chapter 4, ***Marketing,*** *to see how a marketing plan is laid out.*

The following questions are grouped according to function. They are designed to help you organize yourself.

Name and Legal Structure

• Have you chosen a name for your business? If so, will you want to trademark the name?
• Have you chosen to operate as a sole proprietorship, partnership, or corporation?

> **Choose a business.**
> **Choose a business name.**
> **Is the business legal?**

Choosing a Business Structure

Once you decide to establish a business, a primary consideration is the type of business entity to form. Tax and liability issues, director and ownership concerns, as well as state and federal obligations pertaining to the type of entity should be considered when making your determination. Personal needs and the needs of your particular type of business should also be considered. The main types of business entities are:

• Sole proprietorship.
• Corporation.
• Limited liability company.
• Limited partnership.
• General partnership.
• Limited liability partnership.

Sole Proprietorship

A Sole Proprietorship is set up to allow an individual to own and operate a business by him/herself. A Sole Proprietor has total control, receives all profits from and is responsible for taxes and liabilities of the business. If a Sole Proprietorship is formed with a name other than the individual's name (example: John's DJ Service), a fictitious business name statement must be filed with the county clerk or county recorder where the princi-

TIP

To Start a Sole Proprietorship:

1. File a Fictitious Name Statement *(Also known as a DBA - Doing Business As) with the county recorder. This will notify all of your intent to establish a business under your new business name.*

2. Advertise your DBA *in a local paper. You must legally announce that you will be doing business under the fictitious name. Classified ads are fine.*

3. Open a Bank Account: *Take the DBA statement from the county recorder and your published ad to the bank to set up your bank account under your business name.*

pal place of business is located. No formation documents are required to be filed with the secretary of state. The secretary of state is the government agency that controls business entities. Other state filings may be required depending on the type of business and your regional location.

Corporation

A Corporation is defined as a legal entity which separates the liability of the business from that of the owner(s). In other words, the owner(s) of a Corporation cannot be held personally liable for lawsuits filed against the business, and the owner(s) credit cannot be affected by the business debts.

Why Incorporate?

Protection is the chief reason for incorporating. Many people believe that their businesses are too small or too new to incorporate. Others believe that to incorporate would be too expensive. Nothing can be farther from the truth. Here are some benefits of incorporating:

• Provides lawsuit and asset protection.
• Provides tax advantages not available to individuals who obtain businesses or partnerships.
• Avoids personal liability.
• Establishes lines of credit, which are not available to individuals and partnerships.
• Provides easy way to capitalize your business.
• Offers capital for operating expenses.

Limited Liability Company

A Limited Liability Company generally offers liability protection similar to that of a corporation but is taxed differently. Limited Liability Companies may be managed by one or more members. In addition to filing the applicable documents with the secretary of state, an operating agreement among the members as to the affairs of the Limited Liability Company and the conduct of its business affairs is required.

TIP
Nevada and Wyoming corporations have become popular over the past several years because they offer privacy and lower operating costs than offered by many states.

Limited Partnership

A Limited Partnership may provide limited liability for some partners. There must be at least one general partner that acts as the controlling partner while the liability of limited partners is normally limited to the amount of control or participation they have engaged in. General partners of a limited partnership have unlimited personal liability for the partnership's debts and obligation.

General Partnership

A General Partnership must have two or more persons engaged in a business for profit. Except as otherwise provided by law, all partners are liable jointly for all obligations of the partnership unless agreed by the claimant. Profits are taxed as personal income for the partners. Filing at the state level is optional.

Limited Liability Partnership

A Limited Liability Partnership is a partnership that engages in the practice of public accountancy, the practice of law, or the practice of architecture, or services related to accountancy or law. A Limited Liability Partnership is required to maintain certain levels of insurance as required by law.

Your Business and the Law

A person in business is not expected to be a lawyer, but each business owner should have a basic knowledge of laws affecting the business. Here are some of the legal matters you need to be acquainted with. Also, you will find checklists, which are broken out by sections.

• Do you know which licenses and permits you may need?
• Do you know the business laws you will have to obey?
• Do you have a lawyer who can advise you and help you with legal papers?
• Are you aware of Occupational Safety and Health Administration (OSHA) requirements if you have employees?

Do you know about:

• Regulations covering hazardous material?
• Local ordinances covering signs, snow removal, etc.?
• Federal tax code provisions pertaining to small business?
• Federal regulations on withholding taxes and Social Security?
• State workers' compensation laws?

When starting a new business, there are many important decisions to make and many rules and procedures that must be addressed. While there is no single source for all filing requirements, the following checklists have been developed to assist you in starting your business.

Checklists

Federal Government

• Register or reserve federal trademark/service mark.
• Apply for patent if you will be marketing an invention.
• Register copyrights.
• Contact the Internal Revenue Service for information on filing your federal tax schedules.
• Apply for employee identification number with the Employment Department if you have employees.
• Check compliance with federal wage laws.

State Government

• File partnership, corporate or limited liability company papers with the secretary of state's office.
• File state tax forms with the franchise tax board.
• Find out about workers' compensation if you will have employees.
• Apply for sales tax number with the board of equalization if needed.
• Check state wage law if you have employees.
• Observe OSHA safety compliance if you have employees.
• Draft fire egress plan.
• Develop injury and illness prevention program if you hve employees.
• Check compliance with health laws if you have employees.

Download the Ebooks:

How to Get a Tradmark

How to Get a Patent

at the Web site.

Local Government

- Get any required business licenses or permits.
- Order required notices (advertisements you have to place) of your intent to do business in the community. File DBA, (Doing Business As).
- Get local building permit from building department.
- Fire permits - You must pass fire safety inspection if you have a commercial office. Have fire extinguishes? Fire sprinkler system in place? Note: Periodic fire safety inspections will be required after opening.
- Check zoning laws.

Protecting Your Business

It is becoming increasingly important that attention be given to security and insurance protection for your business. There are several areas that should be covered. Have you examined the following categories of risk protection?

- Fire.
- Theft.
- Robbery.
- Burglary.
- Vandalism.
- Accident liability.

Discuss the types of coverage you will need and make a careful comparison of the rates and coverage with several insurance agents before making a final decision.

Business Records

- Are you prepared to maintain complete records of sales, income and expenses, and accounts payable and receivable?
- Have you determined how to handle payroll records, tax reports, and payments?
- Do you know what financial reports should be prepared and how to prepare them?

Other Tasks

• Open a bank account for the business.
• Have menus, business cards, and stationery printed.
• Purchase equipment or supplies.
• Order inventory, signage, and fixtures.
• Get an email address.
• Find a Web hosting company.
• Get your Web site set up.
• Have sales literature prepared.
• Call everyone you know and let them know you are in business.
• Advertise in newspapers or other media if yours is the type of business that will benefit from paid advertising.
• Call for information about Yellow Pages advertising.
• Have business phone or extra residential phone lines installed.
• See if the business name is available for use as a domain name.
• Register the domain name even if you aren't ready to use it.
• Install alarm system.
• If you plan to accept credit cards and bank debit cards, you will need to set up a credit card processing system.

Keep Going...
... Never Quit!

Chapter Notes

_____

_____

_____

_____

_____

_____

_____

_____

_____

_____

_____

_____

_____

_____

_____

_____

_____

_____

_____

_____

_____

_____

_____

_____

_____

_____

_____

_____

_____

_____

_____

_____

Business Plan Primer

Avoid a crash: Plan!

This chapter presents an overview of the basic elements of a business plan. The outline explained here serves as a template for the sample business plan in chapter 5. Study this chapter and then turn to chapter 5 to see how the basic elements of the plan are developed. This chapter also includes information about how to develop your marketing plan, which is part of the business plan.

If you are unfamiliar with financial reports, you might want to jump to chapter 3, *Financial Planning*, in order to become familiar with the financial elements presented in this chapter.

Business Plan Structure

1. Summary.
2. Body.
3. Conclusion.

Executive Summary

This should be an overview and lead-in to the rest of the business plan. It is a summary of the main topics within the plan. It should emphasize your competence in three key areas: Marketing, technical capabilities, and financial management.

The Business Concept

Describe your product or service. Where possible, supplement with diagrams, illustrations or pictures in the final package you show to prospective lenders or investors. This information can be referenced in an appendix.

Marketing Approach

Provide a brief description of your market strategy and the market segment you will be trying to reach. Outline the channel(s) you will use to reach this market, such as direct mail, retail, or wholesale distributors.

Financial Features

Provide estimated dollar amount of sales and net profits that you project for each of the first 3 to 5 years of operation, then set forth the amount of starting capital you will need. Where cash flow is negative (as is usual) in the first few years, it may be helpful to show your net cash exposure or cumulative negative cash flow for each month or quarter, to show that your initial starting capital will be more than sufficient to cover such maximum exposure.

Start-up Costs

Provide a brief overview of the start-up costs. This is basically a digest of the pro forma financial information that you will prepare.

Current Business Position

Provide pertinent information about the company, and whether or not it is a start-up venture: How long it has been in operation. The form of the business: proprietorship, partnership, or corporation.

Achievements to Date

Give an overview detailing any major achievements since the company opened. Provide examples of patents and prototypes. Also, mention where your facility is located. If you are a start-up venture, mention any of the relevant points mentioned above and/or where you currently are in your planning.

Statement of Objectives

Sell your proposal to prospective investors, discussing the unique advantages your product or service has over existing products and services. State both your short-term and long-term business objectives for the business, and describe the image you want to create for your product or firm.

Qualifications of Principals

Provide your background qualifications to run this particular business, citing education, overall business experience and particularly any successful experience in a closely related type of business operation. Also describe, if applicable, the qualifications of your partners or other co-owners who will be part of the management (or board of directors, in the case of a corporation) of your proposed business.

Background of Proposed Business

Spell out the background conditions in the business in question, including how, where, and when the product is being used, as well as where trends in the business or industry seem to be leading. Also, discuss the main players (i.e., your competitors), or likely competitors, if the venture is a start-up operation. Explain where your business will fit in this picture. Will you be on the cutting edge of what is happening, or just one of the pack that is not in the same league as the leaders? If it is the latter, you will need a very convincing rationale to show why you can garner enough business to meet your financial objectives.

Product or Service Use

Provide a complete detailed technical description of the product or service to be offered, including a summary of any test data. Describe any tests that are currently planned. Show that you are anticipating the future by outlining any further refinements or logical next steps for developing an improved or different product later (or comparable plans for further innovations in a service business). This is your chance to show that what you have is a better mousetrap and is also technically feasible.

Industry Overview and Trends

Provide an overview of your industry. Detail any discussions that provide simple graphical representations of the current situation in your industry. Mention any trends that are evident in your industry and/or regarding your products. Through research you can analyze your DJ service and your market potential, helping you make informed decisions.

Information for this part of the business plan is available from two sources:

• Primary research - Collecting the data and compiling it yourself.
• Secondary research - Obtaining the information from already published sources.

Strength and Weakness Analysis

This is where you will do your competitive analysis. Prepare a weighting-scoring model in order to evaluate your key competitors. Primary competitors are in the same business that you are, such as, other DJ services. Secondary competitors would be all other entertainers, such as bands, in your immediate target area. The goal is to rank your business in relation to your competition.

When you know how you rank in relation to your competition, you then can form plans and contingency plans to deal with them.

Basically, the model allows an objective overview of subjective information. It allows you to weight specific criteria and rank the importance of criteria. Score the criteria, then, total the scores.

To see an example of a weighting-scoring model, see the strength and weakness analysis in chapter 5, *The Business Plan..*

Marketing Strategy and Plan

Discuss here your marketing plan or strategy. This will include identifying the market segment you are seeking to reach, and the various means through which you intend to reach it, such as door-to-door sales, retail sales, direct mail, media advertising, selling through sales reps, jobbers, or multi-level distributorships, or whatever else you plan to do. If you can, mention the degree of market penetration and market share you expect to achieve, year by year, for the period for which the business plan is making projections (say 3 to 5 years). Create a budget for all the associated costs and include this in the business plan.

The Four Ps of Marketing

Product

Give a detailed overview of your product(s) and/or services. Include any factors that make it different and why these factors are an advantage to your competitors' product. That will differentiate you in the market place. Illustrate your menu offerings. Define all your products or services.

....

Place

Describe how you will distribute your product or service in the market. Will you reach your target audience by door-to-door sales, retail sales, direct mail, media advertising, selling through sales reps, jobbers, or multi-level distributorships? Describe your primary target location. For example, your DJ service may be located in a underserved region of the county.

Pricing

Describe how you will price your product or service.

Will you use penetration pricing to gain market share or will you price your product as a prestige product, charging a higher price? Are you the only one on the block with this type or product/service? Explain how you arrived at your pricing.

TIP

See page 4.5 for more about market strategies.

For example, when you are operating your DJ service, you might use penetration pricing to drive out a smaller competitor. This "low-ball" pricing strategy can work fine as long as you can still cover your overhead costs. This type of pricing is usually used to increase market share, and is short-term only.

Prestige pricing is used when you want to charge a high price for a high-quality product.

Markup pricing is the most popular method used by wholesalers and retailers in establishing a sales price. When the merchandise is received, the retailer adds a certain percentage to the figure to arrive at the retail price. An item that costs $1.80 and is sold for $2.20 carries a markup of $0.40, or 18% of the retail price. The initial markup is also referred to as the "Mark-on".

Pricing to the competition can be done if it covers your operation costs and still makes a profit. Formula pricing is similar to markup pricing. A fixed value is multiplied by the cost. For example, a restaurant might charge five times the cost for a meal product: 5 x $0.85 = $4.25 selling price.

Psychological pricing is a method to persuade a customer to buy. For example a price of $2.99 for a "value" meal may appeal to a customer who is looking for a discount meal. By charging $2.99 rather than $3.00, the customer perceives value in the product because of the "odd numbered" price. Discount stores and fast-food restaurants use this pricing in conjunction with their primary pricing scheme.

Promotion

How will you promote your product? Discuss in this segment how you plan to go about creating awareness of the product among its ultimate consumers, through advertising, publicity or otherwise, even though most of your sales may be made to middlemen such as wholesalers or retailers.

Cover all methods you will employ, such as telemarketing, circulars, print or electronic media advertising, direct mail, catalogs, or other means. Here it will be useful to include promotion kits, photocopies of dummy ads, brochures or other promotional materials that you may have already prepared, if you feel they will be effective in selling your business plan.

Market Segmentation

Market segmentation is the process of dividing a market into specific differentiated segments that have the same identifiable characteristics so that products and/or services can be designed in order to meet the needs of consumers in each segment. When Henry Ford began producing the Model T, he stated: "They can have it in any color they want as long as it black." His basic marketing strategy was undifferentiated with no segmentation.

Today, car manufacturers recognize a myriad of segments, that taken as a whole, constitute the market for cars. There are segments for hot rodders, mothers with children, young families, status seekers, and even states, whereby government air-quality regulations form a segment.

Forms of Market Segmentation

There are five basic market segmentation forms:

1. Demographic - by age, sex, income.
2. Geographic - by region, urban, or rural.
3. Psychographic - by lifestyle or personality.
4. Benefits - consumer perception: tastes good, feels good.
5. Volume - heavy user, light user.

Organizational Plan

It is important to spell out in a convincing way your plans for structuring the organization, including a description of the key positions and the people who you have lined up to fill them, with their (hopefully impressive) qualifications. Include an operational plan, describing in detail the type, and, if known, location of office and equipment that must be obtained. Also discuss what professional services you will require. For the 3 or 4 key people in the company (including each top person in the sales, finance and technical departments), include their resumes at this point, or place them in an Appendix at the end of the business plan, but refer to them here.

Financial and Technical Data

Here is where you include detailed pro forma financial statements and other important data in support of the conclusions you have set forth in other parts of this business plan. (See chapter 3. *Financial Planning*, for a detailed discussion of these topics). These should include most or all of the following:

Profit and Loss Projection

Profit-and-loss projections should be on a monthly basis for the first 3 years, and quarterly for subsequent years, in most cases.

This projection shows your business financial activity over a period of time (monthly, annually). It is a moving picture showing what has happened in your business and is an excellent tool for assessing your business.

Pro Forma Balance Sheets

These should show your projected ending financial picture for each of the periods covered by the P & L Statement, (Profit and Loss Statement).

The balance sheet shows the condition of the business as of a fixed date. It is a picture of your firm's financial condition at a particular moment in time, and will show you whether your financial position is strong or weak. It is usually done at the close of an accounting period. It contains the following topics:

• Assets.
• Liabilities.
• Net worth.

Download the financial spreadsheet that goes with the sample business plan in chapter 5 from the Web site.

Cash Flow Projection (Budget)

You will need to show monthly or quarterly and cumulative pro forma cash flows, which should tie into the P & L statement and balance sheets for each period covered.

• This document projects what your business plan means in terms of dollars. It shows cash inflow and outflow over a period of time and is used for internal planning.

• It is of prime interest to a lender and shows how you intend to repay your loan.

• Cash flow statements show both how much and when cash must flow in and out of your business.

Break-even Analysis

In chart form or otherwise, show the level of sales you will need each year in order to break even for that period.

The break-even point is the point at which a company's expenses exactly match the sales or service volume.

It can be expressed in:

1. Total dollars or revenue exactly offset by total expenses or,
2. Total units of production (cost of which exactly equals the income derived by their sales).

Acquisition Schedule for Fixed Assets

Show an equipment list and loan-dispersal statement about how and when you plan to acquire your equipment. This can usually be appended to the cash flow budget at start-up.

Other Supporting Data

- Technical drawings of product and/or detailed description of services offered.
- Itemization of capital equipment required and cost.
- Pricing schedule.
- Detailed list of prices for products or services offered, in their different configurations.
- Store layout drawings.
- Floor plans or layout of a proposed manufacturing plant, including a manufacturing flowchart and cost estimates for producing the product, broken down into cost accounting detail.
- Tooling or equipment required for production.
- Description of all tooling that will be required, and the estimated costs.
- Market survey data (primary research).
- Provide any market demographic information that you have developed or obtained.

Summary and Conclusions

This is where you make your final pitch, so make it convincing. Tell what your total capital requirements are and how much of a safety margin that will provide. Describe who will put up what debt and equity capital to get the business off the ground, and when each infusion of capital will be required. This will tell the prospective investors how much of an owner-ship interest they will be getting for X amount of money.

Reiterate the amount of profits you expect the business to make, when you will make it, and how much of your own money and property you are putting into the venture as evidence of your commitment.

Most outside investors are likely to be leery of investing unless it is clear that you have put your own financial neck on the line, so there's no chance of you simply losing interest and walking away.

Appendix

This is where you will include an appendix for supporting data. Include whatever you think will be useful to get your point across. You can have more than one appendix.

This chapter has exposed you to the basic elements of a business plan. The next Chapter, *Financial Planning*, will detail financial elements that you will need to know before you can draft your own business plan.

*Download the Ebook, **The Government Loan Resource Guide**, at the Web site.*

Chapter Notes

_____
_____
_____
_____
_____
_____
_____
_____
_____
_____
_____
_____
_____
_____
_____
_____
_____
_____
_____
_____
_____
_____
_____
_____
_____
_____
_____
_____
_____
_____
_____
_____
_____
_____
_____
_____
_____
_____
_____
_____

Financial Planning

When someone offers you a lifetime warranty, ask:
Whose life, yours or mine?
- Dan Titus

In this chapter we look at financial planning. As a DJ service business owner, you will need to have a basic understanding of the principles presented here. The material presented is from the standpoint of analyzing financial information in order to purchase *any* existing company. This is information you will also use to reinforce your knowledge while you are drafting your business plan. Thanks to Jim Calkins for the use of much of this material from his book, *Business Buyer's Handbook.*

....

Understanding the Health of a Company

The single most important consideration in your review of the company is understanding its financial health. This is done through analyzing and understanding the standard financial measuring tools describing the company. Without knowing how to do this properly, you will invariably ask the wrong questions and get the wrong answers. This, in all probability, will lead to a misunderstanding and possible disaster on your part.

Over the years a standard measurement procedure has evolved for describing the financial health of a company through the use of two health measuring thermometers namely the Income Statement, and the Balance Sheet, or Condition Statement. Both describe the company in very rigid terms representing a fixed time frame.

I present the subjects by going back to the very fundamentals of why you should have financial statements. You may think that you already know how to read a financial statement, but you better be like the major league baseball player who has been playing baseball for fifteen years. Every year he goes to spring training and finds out again and again, that "this is a baseball, and this is a bat, and the fundamental object of the game is to have the bat hit the ball." Most importantly, no matter how long he has played baseball, he learns something new every year. So it is here. You need to go back to the basics and find out what financial statements are and what to do with them. You are bound to learn something you don't already know.

The Income Statement

To understand income and its effect on the company, you have to start with the very basic reason for the business to exist in the first place: Nothing happens until somebody sells something, albeit a tangible product, or an intangible idea. The meaning here is that you are going to transfer something you have to somebody else in exchange for something. Throughout this chapter, that "something" transferred will be either a physical product or an idea, and that "something" received will be interpreted as cash or cash equivalents, i.e. credit cards, money orders, etc.

The term that was created and employed by accountants universally to define that "something received" is income. My definition as used throughout this chapter is:

Income is the total amount of cash or cash equivalents after payment of applicable expenses received from the transfer of goods or services to a second party.

Throughout this chapter I use the term money as a shorthand description of cash or cash equivalents. Each term, money or cash or cash equivalents is used where the occasion requires. But, in every case the meaning is identical.

Critical Basic Point

In studying the financial health of a company, the number one issue is determining the amount of money the company can generate from sales. This number, properly derived, defines whether or not the company is a viable entity worthy of your consideration, or one that needs a considerable amount of TLC, including an infusion of new capital to become and remain viable. The structures and analysis provided below will help you understand how to get this information.

Over the years accountants have developed a standard analysis structure that makes it easy to determine the amount of money available to the company to pay income taxes (taxable income), and the amount of money available to the owner for future use (cash flow).

SALES/ REVENUES
less
Cost of goods sold or cost of sales
gives
GROSS PROFIT
less
Selling expenses
less
Administrative expenses
gives
OPERATIONS INCOME
plus
Other income
less
Other expense
gives

TAXABLE INCOME
less
Income taxes paid
plus
Extraordinary income
less
Extraordinary expense
gives
NET INCOME

1. Sales (Revenues)

These names are used interchangeably by different accountants in the preparation of financial statements depicting the present operations of the company. While there is no universal usage of each, in general, the term sales implies the transfer of a physical item, e.g., product, furniture, food, clothing, tools, etc. for cash, and revenues indicates the transfer of intellectual property such as advice, or knowledge, e.g., legal or other professional advice for cash.

Therefore, manufacturers, retailers, and distributors tend to use the term sales, while service establishments, such as lawyers, accountants, and consultants tend to use the term revenues.

In both cases, the term represents the total amount of cash or cash equivalents received during a defined time from the transfer of goods or services that relate to the primary activity of the entity providing the goods/services, seller, to an entity receiving the goods/services, buyer. (Usage generally excludes interest received, dividends, and incidental gains/losses from the sale of non-primary items.)

2. Cost of Goods Sold (COGS) - Cost of Sales

These are also used interchangeably by accountants to identify those costs associated with the transformation of some form of raw material into a saleable product. These are further identified as direct costs, indirect costs, and inventory. Note: In manufacturing companies, the transformation takes the shape of changing raw material into finished goods via the process of physically making something. In distributorships, the transformation takes the form of handling, storing, and possibly, repackaging in preparation for sale. In some instances with distributorships, the original material may be cut, shaped, and/or rearranged before final packaging for sale. In retail and service companies, the transforming of basic material into a finished product is practically nonexistent. Therefore, the major item in determining the cost of goods sold for these forms of businesses is that of inventory and the costs - both direct and indirect - associated with the handling of the inventory.

a) Direct Costs - Applicable to Manufacturers: All the costs directly related to the physical handling of the materials during the transformation production process, including:

• Raw material purchases, including freight.
• Labor directly connected with the handling of the material through production.
• Outside processors performing specific tasks related to the production process.

b) Indirect Costs - Applicable to Manufacturers: All those costs not directly related to the transformation process, but are identified in the support of the processes. They include:

• Supporting labor (maintenance and repair, truck drivers, etc.).
• Subcontract labor (includes all associated costs).
• Utilities for the shop.
• General supplies and tools for the shop.
• Equipment rental.
• Depreciation - (A non-cash expense allocation). Insurance covering the production process and shop employees.
• Other supporting costs that can be legitimately allocated to production processes.

c) Inventory - Applicable to manufacturers and distributors.

Inventory is defined as a cost summation of all of the physical goods connected with the transformation process, including:

• Raw materials not yet used in the transformation process.
• Materials and goods in the process of being transformed into saleable products. Called Work in Process, or WIP.
• Finished products not yet sold.

With distributors the inventory will consist mainly of finished products not yet sold, and, in some instances, WIP where products are further transformed from the original item into different sizes and packages.

As defined above, for accounting purposes, the cost of goods sold is the total of all costs and expenses directly associated with the transformation of raw materials into the saleable products that were sold during a defined period. To determine this:

Start with the value of the inventory (raw materials, WIP charges attached to the transforming product, and fully transformed finished goods ready for sale) remaining unsold at the end of the last accounting period. This is labeled beginning inventory on the current period income statement. To this, you add all of the costs and expenses rightfully charged to the transformation of raw materials into saleable products during the period, both direct and indirect. Next subtract out the total value of everything that remains unsold at the end of the accounting period, labeled ending inventory on the current period income statement. Note: This is done because what you want is the true cost attached only to those units that were sold during the accounting period. Therefore, you subtract the costs of the ending inventory because you have already paid for them, even though the items were not sold, This figure is now ready to serve as the base for the next accounting period with no additional costs attached, i.e., beginning inventory.

For any given period the cost of goods sold is:

Inventory on hand at the beginning of the period (beginning inventory).
plus
direct and indirect costs identified with the transformation and handling of the saleable products that were sold during the period.
less
cost of unsold materials and saleable products on hand at the end of the period i.e., ending inventory.
gives
cost of goods sold during the period under consideration.

3. Gross Profit

This is a term developed by accountants to determine how much of the sales/revenues money remains after payment of the costs and expenses directly associated with the transformation/production of the saleable product and truly represents what is available to the company for other operations. It is determined by:

SALES/REVENUES
less
COST OF GOODS SOLD
gives
GROSS PROFIT

4. Selling Expenses

Costs and expenses that are directly associated with the physical selling of the finished product are selling expenses. They include:

• Sales salaries and commissions.
• Entertainment and other promotions.
• Travel costs of the salespeople and others.
• Advertising, trade shows, and special events.

5. Administrative Expenses

Expenses associated with the necessary administrative functions of operating the company are administrative expenses. They include all normal and ordinary office expenses, officers' and staff salaries, bonuses, pensions, non-cash expenses, plus payments made to outside professionals, e.g., attorneys, accountants, consultants.

Normally, interest expense is carried in this category, however some accountants prefer to show it as an other expense (defined below).

At this point, it becomes important to explain what is meant by non-cash expenses, and why they are included in a financial statement.

Non-cash expenses are expenses which are allowed by the IRS as legitimate deductions for tax purposes, but for which there is no cash expenditure. These include such items as depreciation, amortization, goodwill, and covenant not to compete. A further explanation of each item is given below:

Depreciation is the recovery over a finite time of the purchase/investment costs of a tangible piece of property, (generally termed a capital item), such as a truck, production tool, desk, etc. that has a limited useful life, and is used on a recurring basis by the company in its normal operations. In as much as the company uses these items on a recurring basis in the normal course of conducting its primary business, and as they have a limited useful life which requires the item to be regularly replaced, the IRS allows the recovery of the acquisition costs over a fixed time period through the mechanism of tax savings. The allowed time for cost recovery is rigidly set by the IRS in published tax bulletins. Generally, the allowed recovery time will vary from 3 to 10 years depending upon the particular item, and how it is used.

Because depreciation does not impact the cash needed to support continued operations, (i.e., no cash has been expended) the amount shown on the financial statement is added back to the income as a non-cash item when developing the amount of cash available to the company for future operations.

Amortization is similar to depreciation in being a recovery of allowed costs. However, in this case the item for which the recovery is made is intangible property such as goodwill, covenants given, and/or recovery of the costs associated with a promise given (promissory note), which are not used directly in the primary operations of the company. Although there is no physical wear and tear on the items, they represent an operational cost for which payment was made, or a value was given. Accordingly, they are allowed full cost recovery.

Since there is no wear and tear, the allowed recovery time will vary from a few (5) years to several (30). Similar to depreciation the allowance time is set by the IRS tax bulletins.

Two of the more important items for which amortization is used are a covenant not to compete, and goodwill, which in all probability, you will use if you purchase your company.

A covenant not to compete is a time-limited promise you will get from the owner of the company you purchase whereby he promises not to engage in a similar type of business representing a direct competition to you for a specific period and within a specific geographic area. The time and area will vary greatly depending upon the type of business and its present location. In general, you will be looking for a 5 to 10 year time limit, and 3 to 10 mile geographic limit.

Goodwill is simply a measure of the intangible value of a company developed over its years in business. Basically it is a measurement of how successful the owner has been at developing good customer relations. A value is given because, in a very real sense, goodwill is payment to the owner for doing the hard work of developing a market and strong customer base.

In accounting terms goodwill generally represents the value of that part of the agreed upon price of the company over the book value of the tangible assets held by the company. (See below for definition of book value.) The assigned value is usually shown in the other category of assets on the balance sheet. (See below for explanation of balance sheet.) Since goodwill does have value, the IRS allows it as a deduction similar to covenant not to compete but over a much longer period of time.

The selling and administrative costs and expenses described above are those normally connected with the day-to-day operation of the company, and when deducted from the gross profit will yield what is called operations income.

GROSS PROFIT
less
SELLING EXPENSE
less
ADMINISTRATIVE EXPENSE
gives
OPERATIONS INCOME

As important as operations income is in defining the health of a company, the term does not give the complete picture of how income totally affects the company. To get the complete understanding of the total amount of income available for tax payment and use in future operations, you must account for those income and expense sources that arise from transactions not normally related to the primary income-earning operations of the company, but are necessary to the overall successful operation of the company. These are other income (expense) and extraordinary income (expense).

Other income (expense) items are distinguished from extraordinary income (expense) by being a part of operating the company, but are not directly associated with the primary income earning activities of the company. They are of a recurring nature. In as much as other income (expense) items are a part of the operations of the company they are added to the operations income before determination of income tax. Examples of other income (expenses) are:

• Interest income.
• Recovery of bad debts.
• Gain or loss from the sale of assets, or gains/losses resulting from investments made on behalf of the company.
• Miscellaneous income/expense.

These also can include:

• Fees paid to Board of Directors.
• Investments made on behalf of the company.
• Special purchases or sales made by the company but which are not part of normal operations.

Extraordinary income (expense) are transactions and events that are both unusual in character and infrequent in occurrence. The transactions and events possess a high degree of abnormality, are unrelated or incidental to the ordinary activities of the company, and are of a type that would not reasonably be expected to recur in the foreseeable future. Because extraordinary items are not an ordinary part of company operations and are non-recurring in nature, all applicable income tax relating to the item must be paid separately and apart from income derived from normal operations. Hence, they are added to the income statement after payment of all applicable income taxes due from normal operations, and are added net of taxes associated with the extraordinary item, if any. That is, after payment of income taxes for the specific item. Thus, you are adding after tax items to after tax items.

Examples are gains resulting from money given to the company from a governmental source for relocation or code upgrade, and losses resulting from major casualties such as fires and earthquakes.

Adding other income (expense) to the operations income will yield the amount of income available to the company for future operations before the deduction for income taxes, termed net income before tax or NIBT. All applicable income taxes due from normal company operations are paid from this income. However, to get the total amount of income available to the company for future operations, after payment of income taxes, the after-tax amount associated with extraordinary income (expense) must be added.

Critical Point

Put a bright Post-it note on this section so you can refer to it quickly. There is no substitute for understanding the financial reporting of a business. The information you gain from Income Statement and Balance Sheet study and analysis lays the foundation upon which all your other investigative data will rest. Financial Reports may seem daunting at first, but don't be put off. Study the reports until you see the story that they are telling. Very soon you will realize the simplicity of their presentation.

For any fixed time period, and from an accounting standpoint, the income available for the company for taxes and future operations is derived by:

Total revenues received during a fixed time period from primary activities
less
Cost of goods sold
gives
GROSS PROFIT
less
Selling expenses and administrative expenses
gives
OPERATIONS INCOME
plus
Other income
less
Other expenses
gives
NET INCOME BEFORE TAX
less
Income taxes
plus
Extraordinary income (after tax)
less
Extraordinary expenses (after tax)
gives
NET INCOME

The term net income, therefore, represents that portion of the total revenues, after taxes, and extraordinary items, that are available to the company for the future ongoing normal conduct of business.

Understanding the concept of income and how it fits into the operations of the company is fundamental to understanding the financial health of the company. Therefore, it is summarized again below:

Critical Point
The word income has been generated by accountants as a tool for the purpose of determining the amount of tax you will have to pay on revenues generated from selling your products or services. The term tells you whether you made or lost money from operations, and how much income tax, if any, you must pay.

As critical as income is to understanding the operations of the company, it does not tell you the number you need most in running your company, namely how much actual cash is available to you from the revenues to successfully operate the company.

Critical Point
Simply put: Cash not income runs companies. Therefore, to determine just how much cash you have after payment of all taxes, you must translate the net income into cash flow.

Fortunately, this process is very simple: Add back those line items that represented a non-cash expense, that is, those line items for which you did not have to write a check, such as: depreciation, amortization, goodwill, and covenants not to compete, etc. that you are allowed (under IRS rules) to deduct as expenses to save taxes.

Accordingly, cash flow is determined by:

NET INCOME
plus
Non-cash expenses:
• Depreciation
• Amortization
• Goodwill
• Covenant not to compete
• Other non-cash items detailed in other income/expense and extraordinary income/expense, that can be legitimately added
gives
CASH FLOW

Therefore, in evaluating the financial health of a company from an income standpoint, you determine how much cash flow is generated from the sales revenues during any specified time period. Typical examples of cash flow generations from healthy companies will be given following the examination of the other measurable aspect of financial health, namely the condition of the company.

Before presenting those items labeled as representing the condition of a company, it is important to describe exactly what is meant by condition so that as you study the various line items you will better understand why they are there, where they came from, and how they impact the operation of the company.

The word condition of a company closely parallels what you mean in describing the condition of your own body. To be in good physical condition means that you have certain body parts (heart, lungs, kidneys, etc. - assets) that must be present to permit you to survive as a living person. All of these parts must be functioning within specified ranges, that is, not being harmfully degraded by foreign entities (liabilities.) Absent these parts within the specified ranges means that you are not in good condition but, in fact, are sick to some degree.

So it is with an operating company. To be in good financial condition means that the company has all of those parts required to function effectively, and that they are within a specified range. Absent any part within its designated range means the company is sick to some degree.

Those parts that an operating company needs (assets) are:

• Cash.
• Inventory.
• Tools and equipment used to perform the transformation from raw materials to saleable products.
• Physical place to perform the transformation from raw materials to a saleable finished product.
• Means of moving the saleable product to the customer.
• Means of collecting the money from the sale of the product.

Those foreign entities that degrade the vitality of the operating parts (liabilities) are:

• Loans and notes owed to outside entities and/or shareholders.
• Taxes and fees owed to local, state, and federal governments.
• Set asides (accruals) for future payments of loans, taxes, etc.

If the operating parts (assets) are not overly degraded by the foreign entities (liabilities) and can remain within a specified positive range, then the company is said to be in good financial condition.

If, on the other hand, the foreign entities (liabilities) seriously degrade or overtake the operating parts, then the company is sick, or unhealthy to some degree.

For accounting purposes, the names and definitions of the operating parts and foreign entities, and the rules for measuring the degree of the health (condition) of a company have been rigidly defined and applied. These are described below.

Balance Sheet or Condition Statement

The balance sheet, or as used by some accountants, the statement of condition describes the financial condition of the company at a specific date. It is a time snapshot of the general health of the company related to its ability to stay in business and remain profitable.

The universally accepted term for the health of the company at any given time is net worth or book value.

> ### Critical Point
> In simple terms, the balance sheet, or condition statement displays the sum of everything the company owns - assets - less the sum of everything the company owes - liabilities. If this difference is positive, then the company has a good chance to grow and be successful. If the difference is small, or negative, then the company is in trouble, and may not survive either in the short or long term.

An examination of the respective portions defining net worth is given below:

> ### Critical Point
> As you read through the upcoming paragraphs and the associated definitions of the numbers generated to help you in your analysis, remember that these were developed by accountants as a means of easily defining the operating health of the company. Over the years, these numbers and their method of presentation have been honed and refined to great detail. Therefore, they represent an accurate snapshot of the company's viability. You should become very familiar with the definitions and usage of each factor as they will carry considerable weight in your understanding of the company. Since they are universally accepted and understood by those who operate businesses, I will use names and attendant definitions throughout this book in describing certain points I wish to emphasize.

Assets

Assets are the tangible and intangible items owned by the company that contribute to its general health. In a human they are the heart, lungs, internal organs, skeleton, and other parts that make up the human body. They are characterized as current assets, fixed assets, and other assets.

Current assets are cash and other acquired resources that are reasonably expected to be consumed or disposed of during a normal operating cycle of the company. They include:

• Cash (On hand in the company, and/or in the bank).
• Receivables.
• Trade sources, less an allowance for bad accounts.
• Non-trade sources.
• Loans receivable from officers and other employees.
• Prepaid payments made on taxes, rent, and loans.
• Inventory.
• Raw materials.
• Work-in-process.
• Finished goods.

Fixed assets are those resources company-owned which are normally not consumed during one operating cycle of the company, are long term in nature, and are active in supporting the operations of the company. Consumption usually takes several years with the costs associated with the resource being recovered for tax purposes through the mechanism of an annual depreciation allowance. (See income statements).

Generally included are:

• Real property (land and buildings) owned by the company.
• Vehicles used in the operation of the company.
• Machinery and equipment used in the operation of the company.
• Tools and dies used in the operation of the company.
• Leasehold improvements on the owned real property that are used in the operation of the company.
• Office furniture and fixtures used in the operation of the company.

Other assets are those resources that normally will not be consumed during the usual operating cycle of the company, and are not active in supporting the operating process. They include:

• Deposits.
• Life insurance, cash value, and goodwill/covenant allocations.
• Investments made on behalf of the company.

The total assets owned by the company are the sum of the three categories:

CURRENT ASSETS
plus
FIXED ASSETS
plus

OTHER ASSETS
gives
TOTAL ASSETS

Liabilities

Liabilities are the obligations owed by the company that detract from the general health of the company created by the assets. In a human they are the bacteria, fungus, and other disease causing things that detract from the general body health. Liabilities are characterized as current liabilities, long-term liabilities, and other liabilities.

Current liabilities are obligations for which payment will require the use of current assets, will probably be paid within one year from the current date, and include:

• Current accounts payables.
• Trade payable - open accounts and invoices billed to the company from vendors that supply the materials and services used by the company in the normal conduct of its primary business.
• Non-trade payables - Invoices billed to the company from vendors not related to the primary activity of the company.
• Loans and notes payable - The amount to be paid within the current operating cycle of the company. Called current portion.
• Commissions payable.
• Taxes payable.
• Accruals of future payments of deferred items, such as taxes.
• Salaries.
• Pension/profit sharing.

Long-term liabilities are obligations for which all or partial payment will be made in more than 12 months from the current date and require the use of current assets and/or the creation of other obligations. They include:

• Loans and notes payable to a bank or institution, less current portion.
• Loans and notes payable to officers and others.

Other liabilities are obligations for which payment will, generally, be made in more than twelve months from the current date and require the use of current assets and/or the creation of other obligations. Other liabilities differ from long-term liabilities because they include special types of obligations not generally connected with loans and notes, but are more associated with deferred payment of tax and other obligations, penalties due, and purchase of assets not directly connected with the operation of the company. The total liabilities owed by the company are the sum of the following three factors:

CURRENT LIABILITIES
plus
LONG-TERM LIABILITIES
plus
OTHER LIABILITIES
gives
TOTAL LIABILITIES

Critical Point

As described earlier, the financial health of the company from the standpoint of the condition is simply the total assets less the total liabilities, or:

TOTAL ASSETS
LESS
TOTAL LIABILITIES
GIVES
BOOK VALUE (NET WORTH) OF THE COMPANY

The financial health of a company from the standpoint of condition is determined by a critical analysis and review of the assets & liabilities of the company. From accumulated practical experience, accountants have developed an easy way to perform this analysis by using financial ratios. These are a series of numbers that use various parts of the assets and liabilities to describe whether or not the company is in good health and can survive and grow, or in bad health, probably will not survive unless there is an infusion of new cash, and, in many cases, a new management team.

Numerous ratios have been developed to adequately describe the operational health of a company. They are used for various analytical purposes. However, there are a few key ratios that will give you the basics of what you need to know immediately about the general health of the company under consideration.

Before proceeding with presenting the actual ratios, an explanation of the ratios, their derivation and interpretation is put forth to enable you to have a complete understanding of exactly what the ratio is saying about the health of the company. The names attached to the ratios were developed by accountants and are universal in usage and interpretation. I will first define a series of important ratios and their universally accepted interpretations, then detail the healthy ranges to be used in your analysis.

There are three major categories of operating ratios defining the financial health of the company. These are:

1. Solvency ratios.
2. Efficiency ratios.
3. Profitability ratios.

Solvency Ratios

Current Ratio

Defined as: the total current assets divided by the total current liabilities.

total current assets / total current liabilities

Interpreted as: an indication of the company's ability to service its current obligations. Generally, the value is greater than 1.0. The higher the value, the less difficulty the company has to pay its obligations and still maintain assets that will permit continued growth. A value less than 1.0 indicates the company is over burdened with obligations the company, probably, cannot pay and is in serious risk of not surviving.

Quick Ratio

Defined as: cash and cash equivalents plus trade receivables divided by total current liabilities.

cash and equivalents + trade receivables / total current liabilities

TIP
Key Business Ratios can be obtained from Dun & Bradstreet. Their report, **Industry Norms & Key Business Ratios**, *is a standard reference for industry. Their ratios are developed and derived from their extensive database. Contact them via their Web site: www.dnb.com*

Interpreted as: also known as the acid test, and defines the company's ability to service its current obligations from its most liquid current assets. In this case, a value less than 1.0 implies a dependency on the unscheduled liquidation of inventory or other assets to cover short-term debt.

Current Liabilities to Net Worth

Defined as: current liabilities divided by net worth (total assets less total liabilities).

current liabilities / net worth

Interpreted as: contrasts the funds that creditors have at risk versus those of the owner. A small number indicates a strong company with minimal risk to the creditor's money, implying a high credit rating and ease of obtaining additional debt. Conversely, a high number indicates a greater risk to creditor's money, a lower credit rating, and difficulty in obtaining additional debt.

Total Liabilities to Net Worth

Defined as: current liabilities + long-term debt + deferred liabilities divided by the net worth.

current liabilities + long-term debt + deferred liabilities / net worth

Interpreted as: contrasts with current liabilities to net worth by adding the effect of the long term debt and interest charges on the ability of the company to satisfy creditors. If this number is substantially higher than current liabilities to net worth by approaching 1.0 or greater, then creditors will question the company's ability to continue to service existing debt, let alone additional debt.

Fixed Assets to Net Worth

Defined as: total fixed assets divided by net worth.

fixed assets / net worth

Interpreted as: an indication of the amount of funds the owner has invested in fixed assets. A high number e.g. greater than 0.75 indicates either, a) the company has low net working capital (assets less liabilities) and, in all probability, utilizes excessive long-term debt to fund the assets, or b) the company is probably not utilizing the assets efficiently and has over-invested itself in fixed assets. In both cases, questions must be raised about the ability of the company to survive in the short term.

Efficiency Ratios

Sales to Trade Receivables

Defined as: net sales over a given period divided by trade receivables at the end of the period.

$$\text{net sales / trade receivables}$$

Interpreted as: measures the number of times the trade receivables turn over in the period included for determining the net sales, normally one year. The higher the turnover, the shorter the time between sale and cash collection. Allows a direct comparison of the company to industry norms. If the number is higher than industry norms then the company has achieved a relatively strong position in its market. That also indicates the quality of the receivables is better than the norms. If the number is lower than industry norms, then both the trade receivable quality, and the company's market position need to be reviewed to determine continued market viability.

Day's Receivables

Defined as: the sales/receivables ratio divided into 365 days.

$$\text{365 days / Sales Receivables Ratio}$$

Interpreted as: the average number of days it takes to collect the trade receivables. A large number (60 days) means the company may have little control over its receivable collections and be forced to use new debt instruments to maintain production.

Sales to Net Working Capital

Defined as: net sales over a given period divided by net working capital at the end of the period.

net sales / net working capital

Interpreted as: indicates how efficiently the net working capital (defined as current assets less current liabilities) is utilized in the production of sales. A low number in comparison to industry norms indicates under-utilization of working capital, while an exceptionally high number makes the company vulnerable to hostile takeovers. (Net sales are the total sales less discounts given.)

Sales to Inventory

Defined as: net sales over a defined period divided by the inventory at the end of the period.

net sales / inventory

Interpreted as: defines how efficiently the inventory is managed. Serves as a guide to how rapidly saleable goods are being moved, and the corresponding effect on cash flow. A low number in comparison to industry norms indicates an unwarranted accumulation of inventory, and a needless expenditure of production funds. An exceptionally high number could signal difficulty in meeting customer demands on a timely schedule by depleting inventory stocks.

Profitability Ratios

There are three profitability ratios that define the company in terms of its financial health and its value as a candidate for your consideration. These are:

Return on Sales

Defined as: net income divided by net sales during the accounting period, which is normally one year.

net income / annual net sales

Interpreted as: the fundamental earnings number and indicates the profits earned per dollar of sales. A number above the industry norms indicates a superior company and one that is extremely healthy. A number below industry norms, while not necessarily indicating a sick company, indicates a need for further examination of the causes of the below averages number.

Return on Assets

Defined as: net income over a given period divided by total assets at the end of the period.

net income / total assets

Interpreted as: the key indicator of the profitability of the company. A high number indicates an efficiently run company, while a small number indicates a poorly run company.

Return on Equity

Defined as: net income over a given period divided by net worth at the end of period.

net income / net worth

Interpreted as: the ability of the company's owners to realize an adequate return on their invested funds. The higher the number, the more valuable the company is to both the present owners and potential buyers.

All of the foregoing in this chapter have been devoted to giving you the essential factors and their definitions as they relate to the health of a company. At the end of this chapter is a table of norms for the indicated industries. I will also give some key personal observations about what constitutes a healthy company, and which you may find useful in your search and analysis.

The industries focused on are:

• Retail.
• Distributors/wholesale.
• Manufacturing.
• Personal service.

Critical Point

A note of extreme caution: within each of the general business categories given below, individual companies will vary significantly. A low income, or ratio, for a given company, may indicate a better business opportunity than one one having a high income and ratio. Always remember, as critical as the financial data are, they are not the only parameters that should influence your final buy, or no-buy decision.

Here are a few of my observations regarding the analysis and purchase of companies obtained from my personal experiences. They are offered in no particular order, simply as additional inputs for your consideration.

1. In general, a strong healthy company will show a gross profit of 40 percent or more. While not necessarily a deal killer, a number significantly less than 40 percent needs to be examined closely before final decisions are made. A small gross profit could be as simple as allocating some expense line items that are normally shown in selling or administrative categories as cost of goods sold, or the company could be over charging of direct labor, material purchases, or leased equipment. In either case, a more detailed examination needs to be made to ensure you know exactly why the numbers are the way they are.

2. Always make sure the seller gives you copies of his financial statements willingly and without a long, detailed explanation of why the various line items show the way they do. Also, he should not hesitate in giving you at least the current and last 3-5 years of statements. Extreme Caution: If the owner says "What do you need statements for? Look at what the company has bought me: a new house, a new car, a boat at Newport, a summer estate in Maine, and put all of my kids through college," then he, with a high degree of probability, is taking unreported money from the company, and/or not showing all legitimate expenses on his statements. In which event you'll be in serious trouble if you take over and try to straighten out the books. In this event: run, don't walk,

because you could easily wind up in trouble with the IRS for something you had no control over.

3. While the statements do not need to be audited and certified by an accountant per se, they should be prepared by a certified public account-ant (CPA). This is critical since a good CPA will not risk his license and ability to make a living by knowingly falsifying data for a client.

4. In addition to the internal financial statements, always get copies of the company's income tax returns and compare them with the financial state-ments. The two documents, in all probability, will show slightly different data because of dissimilar requirements of each. However, the income tax return should include a section on reconciling the two documents. If it doesn't, find out why, and determine how significant the lack of the rec-onciliation is. If both documents are prepared by the same CPA, the rec-onciliation will be in the tax return.

5. You should be able to easily determine from the statements exactly how much the seller is taking from the company.

You will find that the vast majority of business owners you talk with are totally honest, and are anxious to put a deal together. They will give you everything you ask for with little difficulty. Nevertheless, you must always be on your guard until you can verify everything.

Break-even Point

The break-even point is the minimum amount of sales a company must make in order to pay all of its operating expenses, before a profit can be made.

To calculate the break-even point, all that has to be known is what your total overhead is and what your direct costs are as a percentage of sales. The formula is:

$$\text{fixed costs} / 1 - \text{variable costs as a}$$
$$\text{percentage of sales}$$

How to Calculate the Break-even Point

For example, Sam's Restaurant is a sole proprietorship that was expected to gross $200,000 last year.

1. Separate and list fixed and variable costs

Fixed Costs (FC) - Are costs that do not vary with the volume of business. These include items like wages, rent, and utilities.

Variable Costs (VC) - Are costs that vary with the volume of sales of the business. Examples include: Food, condiments, and paper products.

Fixed Costs

Labor	$38,000
Payroll tax	3,800
Insurance	800
Rent	9,000
Accounting	500
Bank service charge	150
Utilities	7,000
Telephone	1,300
Interest	800
Advertising	1,000
Depreciation	1,800
Miscellaneous	1,200
Total Fixed Costs	$65,350

Variable Costs

Food & paper products $77,000

2. Divide total variable costs by total sales:

$$\$77,000 \ / \ \$200,000 = 0.39$$

3. Subtract total variable costs as a percentage of sales from one

$$1 - 0.39 = 0.61$$

To determine the annual break-even point, divide the result into the total fixed cost:

$$\$65,350 / 0.61 = \$107,131$$

5. To find the daily break-even point divide the annual break-even point by the number of days the restaurant is open in a year.

$$\$107,131 / 256 \text{ days} = \$418.48$$

6. Determine if the store is operating above the break-even point:

a) Annually

Annual gross income - annual break-even point

Annual gross income	$200,000
Less annual break-even point	107,131
Total	$92,869

b) Daily

Daily gross income = Annual gross income / total days open

$$\$200,000 / 256 = \$781.25$$

The conclusion is that Sam's Restaurant is operating well above its break-even point.

Chapter Notes

_____
_____
_____
_____
_____
_____
_____
_____
_____
_____
_____
_____
_____
_____
_____
_____
_____
_____
_____
_____
_____
_____
_____
_____
_____
_____
_____
_____
_____
_____
_____
_____
_____
_____
_____
_____
_____
_____
_____
_____
_____
_____
_____
_____
_____
_____
_____
_____
_____

Marketing

Marketing is the cornerstone of any business. It is a key element of your business plan and is key to your ongoing operations. This chapter is designed to introduce you to key marketing concepts and strategies. If you have not already done so, review the section titled, *The Four Ps of Marketing* in Chapter 2, which starts on page 2.5. This chapter expands on that information.

············

How to Create a Marketing Plan

There is one vital tool that stands between success and failure with your business. The marketing plan. Many businesses blindly grope their way to sales while others strategically locate their buyers. It isn't hard to see which will work better.

The plan of marketing your business is far more powerful than it seems. It leads you in a definite direction backed with specific research. Marketing shouldn't be a guessing game. It should be a strategic equation with solutions that propel your business forward.

Lastly, your marketing plan should never end. It is ongoing, not a one-time activity. So exercise your business and it will grow to be strong and healthy.

The main reason business owners don't pull together a marketing plan is simply that they often don't know how. Here is a guide to help you through the process and help you put together a road map to your business goals.

Every marketing plan has these key elements:

1. Defining the business that you are in.

2. Assessing your competition.

3. Marketing strategies.

4. Understanding what your business is and where it fits in.

5. Discovering who your buyers are and then locating them.

6. Reaching your buyers and exercising your plan.

7. Evaluating the results.

Buy a notebook for this specific purpose. Don't get fancy with your marketing plan in the beginning. It's important to let the ideas flow as they will and not be forced to fit into a particular format. Use your notebook to scribble, draw pictures, and take notes until your marketing plan begins to take shape.

After you have the key elements and their structure you can organize them into a nice, tidy format. A marketing plan should be revised subtly every month and drastically every six months, which means that you will always need a notebook on hand. Marketing is a process that once put into action requires tweaking, changing, and downright overhauling to make it perfect. Times change, consumers change, environments change; that means your business must change in order to thrive.

Buy a small tape recorder to talk to in your car and to pop on in the middle of the night when something hits you and it will. Ideas generate ideas. The more you work with your plan, the more your plan will work for you. The problem will begin to be putting all the ideas to use, not coming up with ideas in the first place.

Defining The Business That You Are In

It is important for you to define the business that you are in. The Disney Company failed to clearly define the business that it was in, and as a result in the 1980s its business and stock value suffered. Disney has amusement parks, produces movies and other multimedia products, manages sports arenas, hotels, and much more. However, back in the 1980s there was no clear defining factor that pulled all of these entities together. It was not until CEO Michael Isner announced that, "The Disney Company is in the entertainment business", that the persona of the company changed. Likewise, it is important for you to realize the business that you are in.

a. Are you in the DJ business?
b. Are you in the entertainment business?

The correct answer is b.

A DJ service is an entertainment service. The DJ service is a tool to entertain people.

Assessing Your Competition

Often when we go into business we don't like to think about our competition and because they are the "enemy" we don't really want to acknowledge that they exist or could possibly be doing anything right. The problem with this thinking is that it gives your competition an ever-increasing amount of power.

Smart business owners know who their competition is, what it is doing and if it is lucky, how it is doing it. They know their competitions' motto, its logo, its customer service ideal and how they reach its buyers.

Simply put, they know as much as possible. Don't kid yourself into thinking that you don't have competition.

Trust me, very few new businesses are original. If you are one of those very, very...lucky you, because that is the ideal situation, although still fraught with its own difficulties. So gather your courage, admit to having competition, and let's see what the competition has to teach you and make you more powerful.

First and foremost, identify who they are. This is often easy online by simply doing a search of keywords in the search engines. Who came up? What are they doing that is the same as your business and what are they doing that is different?

Make a list of every single aspect you can discover about your competition. Who are they? Where are they? How do they process sales? What methods of payment do they have?

How fast does their Web site load? What are their meta tag/keywords? Who are their customers and/or agents?

What are they doing better than you? How can you improve on this aspect? What are you doing that is better than they are? How can you shift your niche market so that it isn't exactly the same? What are their prices? How do those prices compare with your own?

Ask and answer every conceivable question you can possibly think of about your competition and try to improve your own business so that you are the only conceivable solution.

Finally, keep your competition in your peripheral vision.

Don't forget they are there. Continue to monitor their business methods. It's your best offensive move.

Overview of Market Strategies

Are you the market leader in your industry? Challenger? Do you plan to use a nicher strategy and deal with segments of the industry currently being ignored?

You need to understand and provide a detailed account of what strategy you will use and how you will implement it. The following is an overview of basic market strategies.

Market Leaders

The market leader is the main player in any market with the most market share - the biggest piece of the total pie. For example, Coca-Cola Company is the market leader in the soft-drink industry and McDonalds is the leader in the fast-food market. The primary objective of dominant players is to remain number one. This objective may be accomplished through:

1. Expanding the total market size.

- **New users** - Target customers outside of primary market segment.
- **New uses** - Music for unconvential events: Boat parades.
- **More usage** - Frequent visitor promotions.

2. Protecting current market share.

- **Innovation strategy** - Introduces new product ideas. Is the leader in promotional strategies. Takes the offensive against all competitors.
- **Confrontation Strategy** - Engages in price wars, promotional wars. Succeeds through intimidation.
- **Harassment Strategy** - Hires away key people, bad mouths, applies political pressure, and other illegal or unethical practices, including under-the-table hardball.

3. Expanding its present share of the market.

Profitability tends to increase with market share. It is better to have 90% of the 10%. A difference of 10% in market share may be accomplished by a difference of about 5 points in pre-tax return on investment (ROI).

Businesses with market shares above 40% earn an average ROI of 30%, approximately three times that of firms with shares under 10%.

However it is expensive for the dominant firm to increase market share in a market where it is already the clear leader. Furthermore, other competitors in the market will fight harder if they are facing a diminishing market share.

Market Challengers

Market challengers are firms that occupy the second, third, or fourth place in an industry. They are "runner-up" companies. Examples include: Pepsi Cola Company and Wendy's Restaurants. Runner-up firms must attack the leader or another runner-up firm if they are to increase market share. The market challenger has three basic strategic alternatives:

1. **Direct Attack** - They can go right for the leader, perhaps with direct product discounts or with a promotional campaign.

2. **Back-door or Blindside Strategy** - Basically the challenger "runs" around the dominant firm rather than attacking it directly. For example, the challenger specializes in tight retail markets that the leader will ignore because the region doesn't meet its traffic requirements.

3. **Guppy Strategy** - Attack a smaller competitor and obtain market share at its expense rather than taking on the market leader. If a smaller restaurant goes out of business, then market share can be increased.

Within each of these strategic alternatives the market challenger has a number of tactical alternatives:

• Discounting Price - Equal value but lower price.
• Lower quality - Lower quality of service but much lower price.
• Prestige - Higher quality, higher price.
• Concentration - Greater concentration. Example: More DJ rigs.
• Distribution Innovation - Develop a new channel of distribution. Example: DJ truck.
• Intensive Promotion - Similar to price war but with advertising and sales blitzes as the primary focus.

Market-Nichers

Unless you have millions dollars to launch your business, consider a market-niche strategy. Market in such a way that you become irresistible to your buyers. For instance, instead of selling water, sell bottled water in 10 different flavors. The best flavored, most nutritious bottled water in the world. Now you have a niche. When people think of flavored water, they will think of you.

Make notes. Where can you slice the pie so that what you are doing is specialized and therefore separates you from the masses? Every business has a niche possibility. Consider what yours are. Instead of selling gifts, sell candles. Instead of selling books, sell cookbooks. Get the idea? Now play with it and see what you come up with. What can you do to sliver off a niche of your market and then specialize in it?

Almost every industry includes a number of minor firms that operate in some segment of the market to avoid clashing with larger competitors. An example is Shasta Cola and private label colas found at local grocery stores. The ideal market niche would have the following characteristics:

- Profitable size.
- Growth potential.
- Neglected by major players in the market.
- Defendable against major players in the market.

Some examples of how a market-nicher can be successful are:

- Locate in underserved markets - Inner city.
- Specialize on specific segment - Weddings and school events only.
- Focus on one market segment - Corporate business events.
- Customized service - Mobile DJ truck with sound system.
- Service features - Better equipment and show.
- Unique location - Underserved, neglected region.
- Usage Segmentation - Based on light users versus heavy users. This is an example of the 80/20 rule of business, whereby 80% of business will come from 20% of the customers. The goal is to find the other 20%. In the case of your DJ service, find the 20% that are not repeat customers of established businesses. Then, address this population with a promotional campaign.

The market-nicher is a practitioner of the concept of market segmentation, utilizing multiple dimensions in the delineation of markets.

Discovering What Your Business Is and How It Fits In

This is very important. Your business is a small business. That doesn't mean it won't become a big business. It might even grow to become a corporate business. But right now, it's a small business. You wouldn't put adult size clothes on a toddler. Don't do the same to your business. In the same way that adult clothes would not fit a toddler, so corporate-sized solutions won't fit your small business.

Make the most of what you are. You can't mass advertise like your corporate other, but you can reach targeted audiences through articles in the right publications. You can overcome corporate deep pockets by acting like a small business and offer human solutions, more service, friendliness, one on one, and much more. Understand who you are and develop your strengths. It will be your strengths that pull you away from your competitors and differentiate your services.

Discovering Who Your Customers Are and Locating Them

So who are they? Who, specifically are the people who would buy your product or service? Start with what you are selling and answer the obvious. Yes, in your notebook. Are you selling baby clothes? Then your buyers are most likely to be women between 20 and 35.

How expensive are the baby clothes? If they aren't expensive then your buying audience may be younger, couples with less money. Blue collar workers. If the baby clothes are quite expensive, then your audience might be dual working couples in an older category. Professional white collar couples. See how this works? Define what you know about your potential customers. Understand who they are personally and their habits. Evaluate what income bracket they might be in. What do they do in their spare time? What magazines do they read? What newspapers? Think like a potential customer.

Help yourself out by subscribing to the trade publication specific to your business. Every single industry has one, even funerals! Find yours by going to the local library or, better yet, university library and seeking out directories of trade journals. This will become an invaluable resource for staying on top of selling trends and what your buyers are doing.

Join online groups that share an interest surrounding the service or product of your business. This is where niche marketing will really help you out because people love to talk to people who love all the same things they do. Follow them. Listen to them. Join them. And learn from them.

Buy books about your trade, buy mainstream magazines around your trade, buy the publications that your competition advertises in, and read, read, read. This is immensely important as it teaches you about your buyers. Keep a healthy section of your notebook about all the things you learn about your buyers and finding them will become easier and easier. You have to know who they are. You have to understand them before you can find them and sell to them.

TIP
You can locate potential customers online by using Internet search engines. One favortie is: www.google.com

Join a DJ trade association. See appendix for listing.

Reaching Your Buyers and Exercising Your Plan

Now you know who your buyers are and you're learning more about them everyday. The next question is how will you reach them? What methods will you employ to get your service in front of them? Online businesses have several avenues including:

Internet Newsgroups and Mailing Lists

Join the lists that include your buying audience. Participate wisely by supplying valuable information and responding to requests quickly. Always use an email tag and your Internet address as this will serve as your ad.

Email Advertising

Purchase opt-in advertising. Opt-in advertising is where people agree in advance to be involved in the email list by permission. You can customize a sales pitch that goes directly to the email boxes of your targeted buying group.

Newsletter Advertising

Advertise in newsletters whose subscribers are your buying audience. In other words, the people most likely to be interested in your service or product.

Article Writing and Ezine Submission

Write and submit articles to newspapers and magazines. Don't forget Internet Ezines, which are Internet magazines. All readers may potentially be interested in your products or services.

Write a Newsletter

Write, maintain, and build your own subscriber base by writing a weekly or bi-monthly newsletter.

Create a Web Site With Reciprocal Links

Create a Web site and exchange links with Web sites that compliment, but don't compete, with your business. Network!

Strategic Alliances

Align yourself with people who can push your product or service for you, who will stand behind you by referring business to you.

Yellow Pages and Word of Mouth

Place an ade in the Yellow Pages. Research your competition there. Encourage word-of-mouth referrals by asking your clients who they know that would be interested in your services or products.

Press Releases

Get the word out regularly to the media. Article space in publications out performs ad space ten times over.

Business Cards

Every time you go out make a point of giving out at least 3 business cards. Make sure your Web site address is clearly and boldly printed on it. If possible, use both sides of your business card. Be creative.

Direct-Mail Copy

Put together a direct mail package about your business and mail a predetermined number of copies to targeted groups each month. See promotion tips on the next page.

Inform clubs, associations, organizations, and intrested entities about what you do. Offer them special discounts. In the end it will pay you back tenfold.

Now that you have some ideas about how to reach your buyers, put together a plan that you will follow without fail every single week. Persistence builds momentum. Stay with it and the sales will be yours.

Create a Power Point Presentation

Portable computers are a great way to showcase your material. Simply create a Microsoft Power Point presentation, and show this to your prospective customer. This software, which is basically an electronic slide show, is easy to learn.

Evaluate the Results

Finally evaluate the results of your marketing efforts. Consistently ask your clients how and where they heard about you. Keep a detailed record of which marketing methods are bringing in the most business and give more attention to the winners. Marketing takes diligence and observation.

Drop the methods that are not performing and increase methods that are working well. Don't make a decision based on one ad. For instance don't drop newsletter advertising if the first campaign doesn't work. Make a decision based on 10 ads. Then if it doesn't work, look to other newsletters that might bring in better results rather than dropping the newsletter method as a whole.

DJ Service Promotion Tips

First impressions are everything. You only get one chance to make them, then it's over. Being ready at all times is the key to advanced sales. If a potential customer asks about your service you must be prepared to hand them a business card and if possible a brochure. You can be the best DJ in the world, but if you are not ready for opportunities, you will starve. A professional image is a must for any DJ service. Therefore, it is important to spend some time putting together your primary offensive sales tools:

1. Business cards.

Business cards are your first line of offensive attack. Always have plenty of them with you at all times. They are cheap and are a great way to promote your business. You can pass them out at most any occasion and the business that they generate is invaluable.

2. Promotion kit.

Your second line of offensive attack is your promotion kit. Promotion kits are traditionally pocket portfolios. The pockets have space for pictures, promotion brochures, and price sheets. Although these make for a nice presentation, I recommend that you budget the money for a full-color brochure. Brochures provide a degree of professionalism, which can help with your overall promotion efforts. They are much cheaper to mail. Therefore, you will save money in the long run.

Good promotion text copy must contain a brief biography of your business and how long you have been in business. A good biography must answer these questions:

Q: Who are you?
A: Your DJ service name.

Q: What kind of service do you provide?
A: Professional DJ entertainment services.

Q: Why are you in business?
A: To help satisfy demand for DJ entertainment services.

TIP

Brochures are expensive to print and can become obsolete if contact information changes. Therefore, put your contact information on your bio and/or price sheet. Reference the reader of your brochure to these documents. For example, "See our price sheet or Web site for current contact information."

Q: Where are you located?
A: List the city in which your primary office is located and all contact information, including: address, telephone number, and Web site address.

Q: When are your services available?
A: Outline briefly when your service is available. Example: Weekend events and holidays only.

Stress the benefits that your service provides. Examples might include:

• Professionalism: Number of years in business.
• Top show performed: Celebrity events.
• Equipment: Name brand sound systems and lighting systems.
• Program material: Large, varied selection of music.
• Top references and endorsements: Quotes from satisfied customers.
• Pricing: Economical pricing.

A good promotion kit will have a video tape or DVD that will showcase your material. With the advent of digital video and price drops for computers and editing software, production of these kinds of materials is becoming very economical. A short 10-minute presentation is all that is needed and will provide a potential customer an overview of your services.

3. Your Web site.

Your Web site is a basic extension of your business and in many cases the first contact with potential customers. Mirror your company persona across your Web site. Use the same graphics at your site that you use in your other promotional materials: Company logo artwork. This will reinforce your DJ service in the mind of consumers every time they see it.

Always ask if the contacts have Internet access. If they do, invite them to visit your Web site - if they have not been there previously. If they have specific questions that can be answered at the site, direct them to it. Be sure to get their contact information before you refer them, so that you can place a follow-up telephone call at a later date.

Direct Sales

Qualify Your Potential Customers

Time is money and money is time. Therefore, it is important to budget the time that you spend with customers. You need to qualify each sales call so that you can proceed with closing the sale. You can screen your sales calls with these questions:

• How did you hear about us?

Use this question to gauge and measure your promotion efforts. Record the respondents answer on a tick sheet that can later be tabulated in a spreadsheet. Your goal with this question is to find out how your promotion efforts are working by measuring the results. For example, if you passed out 200 brochures at a school event and you received 25 telephone calls as a result, your cost per lead generated would be the total cost of the flyer, divided by the number of calls:

Measure Your Cost Per Lead

cost per lead = cost of flyers / number of telephone calls

cost per lead =

(200 flyers x .07 copy charge + ad development charge) / 25 calls

$14.00 copy charge + $40.00 = $54.00 total flyer costs

$54.00 / 25 = $2.16 per lead

Use a code number on your promotion media so that you will know where sales leads are generated. For example, you can buy a cheap numerical rotary stamp and stamp your flyers with a specific code number in a box predetermined on the flyer. When customers call and mention that they have a flyer, ask them for the promotion code, and then log it. Thus, you have a control point on your cost-per-lead program. You can use this same method for display ads:

Cost for ad / number of calls

$375 / 50 calls = $7.50 per lead

• What is your budget?

This question is designed to filter the respondents willingness and ability to pay for your services. They may be willing to purchase your service; however, they may not be able to pay for it and vice versa. They may be able to pay for your service, but be unwilling to pay the price that you are asking. If you charge $400 for a minimum 4-hour event and the customer can't afford it, send them a brochure so that they will have your contact information for next time. It is not necessary to contact them again, except for mailings from your mail list and direct-mail campaign. Let them contact you.

If a respondent has an established budget that meets your minimum service requirements, you have a solid lead that warrants investigation. If the person begins by asking for a price concession, you must deal with the objection. Remember, you have a solid lead with this kind of respondent. You can deal with price objections by touting your service benefits, which are outlined in your promotion kit or brochure.

Close the Sale

Once you overcome all objections, it is time to close the sale. You must still get the business. Ask, "Are you ready to get started?" If the answer is yes, send them a brochure and contract to return along with the appropriate deposit.

Marketing Feedback and Improvement

When you close the sale, you are not finished with your marketing effort. You need to continuously improve your service. One way to do this is by providing a customer survey questionnaire. Your survey should have questions to rate your performance and at the same time query the customer as a reference. If the survey is a favorable one and the customer agrees to act as a reference for your service, you win a valuable resource. Provide the survey at the end of each job or mail it to the customer. It is best to get the customer to complete the survey form immediately at the end of the job. This will increase your chances of getting the information back with no follow-up necessary. Follow-up calls cost money.

Typical Customer Questions

Here are some typical questions that customers have. Use a defensive sales strategy by being ready for customer questions and objections in advance. Write additional questions that they might have, and come up with a FAQ (Frequently Asked Question) sheet that you can give to each customer in advance. Include this sheet as part of your promotion kit.

May I see a performance?

You can send a video tape, DVD, or show a Power Point presentation; however, they sometimes only tell half the story. They are a great way to introduce your service to potential customers and prequalify them.

Use this option for hard-to-close customers: If the customer asks to see a live performance, try to accommodate the request within your schedule. Suggest that they come see your performance only if time permits and if the event coordinator of the job allows it. It is rude to invite uninvited guests to any event. Use this opportunity to close the deal firsthand.

What kind of experience do you have?

Most DJs with more than 50 shows' experience are going to know what to do at an event. This coupled with a show action plan will be your keys to success. Your professionalism here will pay off. Offer to send a brochure or complete promotion kit if you feel it is necessary. Follow-up with a telephone call. Ask, if there any questions that you can answer. Proceed to close and book the sale.

Do you have a varied music selection?

How many songs do you bring to your shows? What format? A top professional should exhibit a sizeable song list (at least top 2,000 songs for shows requiring 1940s to current Top 40 mix). Your DJ service should have the styles of music the customer wants. If you don't have a song list, offer to show your CD collection. The best approach is to catalog your collection in a database. Most professional DJs have song lists using software like Music Database 2000 or something similar.

Do you have references?

References are standard with any promotion kit. If you are asked for references send a brochure with reference information or direct them to a page on your Internet Web site. Keep the URL for this page unlinked so that you can direct them to it verbally because you don't want to bother your references with too much traffic. For example, a URL might look like this:

www.jimandjudysdj.com/references.htm

Once they have the information contact them within a few days with a follow-up call to close the sale.

Do you provide a written contract?

It is very important to confirm your booking in writing. Terms should be clearly defined to avoid future problems. It is simple to refer a potential customer to a hidden page at your Web site that has this information if they insist on seeing it in advance.

Do you have liability insurance?

This is an important question and one that you should be ready for. Refer the potential customer to an unlinked page on your Web site, or send a current copy of your insurance policy for review if requested.

Will you listen to my music suggestions?

Many DJs are of the opinion that they know what music is best for their audiences and won't take requests. The DJ should listen to requests and play them whenever appropriate. This is quelled by your preplanning action plan, which includes a music request sheet provided by the customer. See page 7.3 in chapter 7, *Operations,* for an example of a music request sheet.

TIP
Update your references often. People have short memories. Therefore, you want references that are current and still excited about your DJ service.

How will you dress for my event?

It is important to query potential customers about their needs. You must dress the part by dressing formal, semi-formal, or casual, according to your customers' preference. However, be sure to inform them that themed events and special costumes will require additional coordination and therefore, most likely additional costs.

Do you have backup equipment and backup personnel?

Even professional audio equipment can fail on occasion. Don't let this put an early end to your event. Make sure there is backup equipment and be sure there is a backup DJ should an emergency or illness occur.
You can make arrangements with a competitor if you do not have additional personnel resources.

Will you play music at the appropriate level?

A prime concern voiced by prospective clients is the volume level of the music. A professional DJ keeps the volume at a level appropriate for the guests, especially during cocktails and the dinner hour. In today's sue-happy society, it is best to be safe. If you damage someone's ears because of negligence due to sound volume, expect a lawsuit.

Do you provide services other than music for the event?

Most events involve more than playing music. It is important to offer basic announcement services. Your event planning sheet can help with this because the customer will provide you with specific information in advance.

TIP
See page 7.2 for an example of a event planning sheet.

See the appendix for listing of DJ associations.

Do you belong to a professional DJ association?

If you belong to a professional DJ association, tell people. This will add to your professional persona and increase your credibility. There are several associations that offer services that can assist with your endeavors.

The Business Plan

It's sad, but many people are not exposed to the concept of a business plan until going for their MBA (Masters in Business Administration) in college. If I had my way, students would not be able to graduate high school without at least a basic understanding of the elements of a business plan.

In this chapter you will find a sample business plan. Be sure to read Chapter 2, *The Business Plan Primer,* and Chapter 3, *Financials*, so that you will have the necessary footing to draft your own plan using the plan represented here as an example.

Studies indicate that one of the primary reasons that a start-up business fails is because no business plan was developed, and more importantly, implemented. A business plan is basically a road map so that you know where you are going. Many people, and many consultants, believe that a business plan is nothing more than an equipment list and basic costing information. While these are certainly important, they are only very small pieces of the whole puzzle.

Business Plan Benefits

Some of the business plan benefits are:

• Provides you with an operating blueprint.
• Assists with the financing of your business. Your banker or investor will insist on seeing your plan.
• Assists with your negotiations with agents, event planners, and campus personnel.
• Provides a powerful business navigation tool. Defines the business goals and objectives. Allows for plan adjustment - Make your mistakes on paper, it is cheaper!
• Provides a powerful negotiation tool.

If you have ever drafted a business plan, you know that it is a major feat. No one can draft a better plan than you. Sure, there are professionals that can do it for you; however, you are the best person to judge for yourself the current status of your own desires, goals, and financial situation.

There are many stand-alone computer programs on the market that promise a business plan in just hours. While these programs are good at providing general insight into business, they will not provide you with the research necessary to complete a detailed business plan. Can you imagine one of these programs doing a good job if your chosen business happens to be chicken farming in New Zealand? Or, if your chosen business is a mobile DJ operation?

You can waste a tremendous amount of time trying to take the easy way out. There is really no simple way. You need to participate in your own future by doing a business plan for yourself or providing the necessary information for a professional consultant to do it.

If you do not have the time or resources to do your own plan, be prepared to spend between $2,500 and $3,500 to have the plan prepared for you.

Depending on the amount of research, this fee can go even higher. The outline used in this plan is simple. Most business plan outlines are similar. However some are just too detailed and verbose for my liking. My strategy is KISS i.e., keep it simple stupid (an acronym used by business people).

This sample business plan will provide you with a template to start constructing your own business plan. Take your time and study the table of contents outline; then, thumb through the plan to familiarize yourself with some of the topics.

Where do I start?

You begin with the business plan financials because the bulk of the plan is written directly from the financial schedules. For example, the Financials Features Section is derived directly from the Pro Forma Income Statements. Pay attention to the assumptions on this schedule - and all of the other financial schedules because they document the thinking behind the numbers. Study the cell formulas of the financial spreadsheets to see how the assumptions tie into the overall statement. You can use the financial statements in this plan as a model or build your own. Remember that the financial portion is the backbone of your plan. Start with financials and then write the rest of your plan.

This is a Project

You have to look at this as a project. You must break the project down into manageable steps given your most precious current resource: Time. As aforementioned, start with the business plan financials. Once you start, you will find that the sales forecast numbers feed the revenue portion of the Pro Forma Income Statement on the spreadsheet. In other words, when numbers are input into the sales forecast, they are automatically posted to the Income Statement. Next complete the expenses part of the Income Statement i.e., cost of goods sold, operating expenses, and taxes. Then, you will be two thirds of the way done with the financial section.

In the meantime, begin to construct the body of the business plan. Start your marketing plan. Study your primary competition - the services in the same business that you are in. Study your secondary competition - bands and other forms of entertainment. Plan your attack. Think about your

You can get get sample financial spreadsheets at the Web site.

Project management task scheduling software is available at the Web site. Use this electronic "To-do list" to budget and keep on track!

business concept. All of these questions can be answered and plugged into the text body of your plan while you are working on other parts of the plan. If you have a number of partners, assign each of them different portions of the plan. Take advantage of the skills of the people in your group; maybe there is an accountant or a marketing specialist. If so, use those skills.

Your business plan is basically an educated guess in many ways. That's the whole idea. You are minimizing risk by creating a plan; that's what pro forma means. It's a forecast, an educated guess. It's in your best interest to put everything on paper so that any mistakes can be made on paper where they are much easier - and cheaper - to correct.

Enter Murphy. Murphy's Law states: "... if anything can go wrong it will." Try to anticipate anything that can go wrong in advance. Identify these fail-points. Don't be afraid to offer one, two, or three back-up plans. For example, you might say "... we have identified a shortfall in revenues in the third quarter in year 2. However, observations have shown that the county fair is in operation for 12 weeks during this same period. We have forecast sales based on the demographics derived from the fair population, and believe that we can post an added gross based on 4 additional gigs that we can obtain."

The important thing is to answer all of your questions and above all, answer all the questions to the best of your ability. That way you will have confidence in your plan when you are finished.

Sample Business Plan

The remaining pages illustrate a sample business plan that you can use as an example to create your own plan. This plan follows the same format presented in Chapter 2, *The Business Plan Primer.*

Download this sample business plan from the Web site. In popular Microsoft Word format, you can use this as a template to create your own business plan. Also available is the Microsoft Excel spreadsheet that was used to create the financials that go with this business plan. You can edit this information, too.

Executive Summary

The validity of this business concept, as exemplified in this plan, illustrates a strong potential for success. The plan communicates leadership ability by its operators as evidenced by their business and educational experience. The plan's strong marketing analysis and financial features further identify the operators' business and technical abilities.

The mobile DJ business is poised for long-term growth. Therefore, we see a trend in this area for several years. Growth potential is the essence of this plan because it secures a revenue base from which to operate and profit returns for the future.

The Business Concept

Jim & Judy's DJ Service will open with the primary goal of providing entertainment. Market niches will include weddings, parties, corporate business, and special events.

Marketing Approach

We will reach our market through mobile services by traveling to appropriate job destinations. Our primary promotion tools will consist of co-op advertising, display advertising, direct-mail advertising, and personal selling.

Financial Features

Pro Forma financial statements have been prepared for the first 3 years of operation and include: Income statement, Balance Sheet, Monthly Cash Flow, Cash Flow, Revenue Estimates, and Depreciation Schedules. Three-year annual profit-and-loss summaries have been prepared, which exemplify revenue growth and marginal increases in the cost of doing business.

The summary of annual profit and loss is as follows: Year 1 start-up annual profit after taxes is estimated at $39,565 on total revenues of $68,200. Totals for years 2 and 3 show revenues of $81,550 and net profit after taxes of $48,527 for both years because we do not anticipate oper-

NOTE
*Year 1, 2, and 3
in this example
would be sequen-
tial years in your
business plan.
For example,
2007, 2008, and
2009.*

ating increases. Therefore, these years are basically flat.

Summary Figures ($)

Year	1	2	3
Revenue	68,200	81,550	81,550
Gross	65,440	78,210	78,210
NIAT	40,015	48,537	48,537

All forecasts are predicated on data gathered from studies done from observations and personal interviews with event planners, agents, school coordinators, and DJ services in the area.

Start-up Costs

Total start-up costs are estimated at $12,365. This figure includes $9,765 for equipment, $1,000 for initial promotion and first installment payment of $6,00 for liability insurance, which is $1,200 annually. See page 5.19 *Start-up Cost Schedule*, for details.

Current Business Position

Jim & Judy's DJ Service is a new start-up venture, which will be operated as a sole proprietorship by Jim and Judy Johnson. The purpose of the business is to provide entertainment services. This plan outlines the validity of this venture by providing a review of the current market, and presents our business concept. We have $14,000 of capital investment for this start-up venture: $9,000 from personal savings and $5,000 from a secured equity loan on our property.

Achievements to Date

- Marketing concept has been developed.
- Capital funding has been secured.
- Equipment has been specified and selected.

It must be stressed that Jim and Judy will be putting up $9,000 from personal savings, thereby giving them a significant equity situation from the start.

Statement of Objectives

We plan to improve on the existing and successful operations already in the marketplace. There are many DJs in the area. However, we know through our research that the majority of these services are not our direct competition because they only cater to an occasional teen party or high school dance. We have developed short- and long-term objectives

Short-term Objectives

- Produce enough revenue to cover costs of operation.
- Create customer awareness of our service.

Long-term Objectives

- Our goal is launch and then refine our concept for the first year. The first year is planned as a proving ground.
- If our concept, financial estimates and planning are on target, we plan to expand the service within a few years.

Qualification of Principals

Jim Johnson, who is currently employed by Randolph Construction, has more than 10 years experience as a manager in manufacturing operations. Jim holds a bachelor of science degree in business marketing from California State University, San Diego, California. Jim has been trained in TQMS (Total Quality and Management Techniques) and has implemented/participated in continuous improvement as part of his management philosophy. Jim is an accomplished musician and entertainer who has worked for local night clubs and DJ'd since his teen years.

Judy Johnson, who is currently employed by The Sam Martin Corp., Long Beach, California, has more than 10 years experience in the computer field as a programmer and analyst. She holds an associate degree from Cerritos College, Cerritos, California, and is an accomplished singer and dancer. Judy began to work as a DJ when she was a freshman in high school and has done hundreds of gigs - jobs.

Background of Proposed Business

More and more clients are relying on mobile DJ services as the primary form of entertainment. Weddings, corporate functions, private parties, and school functions all currently use DJ services. Therefore, the industry is in a steady growth mode. There is increased competition in the industry; however, this competition is fragmented based on:

• Experience.
• Professionalism.
• Business stability.

The players in this arena are primarily competitors who are divided into three camps:

• **Part-time under 18 year old DJs:** Their target market is private parties and school functions. These are mainly hobby people in the business for fun.
• **Part-time DJs over 18 years of age:** Their target market is weekend functions: Weddings, business functions, private parties, and school functions.
• **Full-time DJs over 18 years old:** Their target market includes weekend functions, such as weddings, school functions, private parties, and business functions. They also will travel more and do these kinds of functions during the week. These DJs also may work dance clubs, which have permanent sound and lighting installations.

We will concentrate our efforts in the part-time DJ over 18 category. We plan to work weekend jobs for the most part. We will differentiate ourselves by offering a degree of professionalism not offered by our competitors.

Industry Overview and Trends

There are currently no industry figures available for the DJ industry. However, we feel given time, professional DJ associations will supply industry data as a service to their membership. We have questions. For example:

• What is the total market in dollars for DJs in the United States?
• What is the total market share in dollars for the major players in the market, versus total market share in dollars of all independents?

Strength and Weakness Analysis

Primary Players

We have used a weighting-scoring model to analyze the competition as well as analyze ourselves.

CRITERIA	WEIGHT(%)
Years in business	20
DJ experience	25
Marketing experience	20
Entertainment experience	10
Financial experience	5
Financial resources	15
Technical experience	5
TOTAL	**100**

Basically, the model allows for an objective overview of subjective information. It allows you to weight specific criteria that ranks its importance; score the criteria, then, total the scores. The score range is 0-5. The final scores are placed on a scale, which is made by multiplying the lowest score and the highest score. Competitors were scored based on observations and assumptions. Our analysis ranks the market players as a weight percentage.

The overall goal here was to see how we stack up against the competition. The scores for all players, including our company, are on the next page.

We have identified three competitors in our area:

1. Terry's DJ Service is a part-time under 18-year-old service. It has been in business for 1 year and is owned by Terry Edwards, a teenager. Terry has 2 years experience as a DJ and performs for intermittent school dances and occasional private parties. He does not operate his company as a business entity and is in the business, at this time, simply for fun. This business scored a 1.25 on our weighting-scoring model out of a maximum score of 5 points. Therefore, we do not see this business as a major competitor in our market.

2. Astro Entertainment is a full-time over 18-year-old sole proprietorship that has been in business for 3 years. The owner, Bill Savage, has 4 years direct DJ experience. Bill operates a single DJ rig. Astro scored a 3.25 on our model. Therefore, we see that Astro is a viable competitor in our market.

3. Party Plus is an event planning agency that has an entertainment division. This corporation books events and draws from its division talent pool first before it books secondary talent. It has been in business for five years and currently has 4 full-time employees dedicated to DJ entertainment functions. The combined DJ experience is over 12 years. Party Plus scored a 4.25 on our model. Therefore, we see it as a viable competitor in our market.

4. Jim and Judy's DJ Service scored a 3.30 on the model. Here are the summary results:

WEIGHTING-SCORING MODEL	
BUSINESS	**SCORE**
Terry's DJ Service	1.25
Astro Entertainment	3.25
Party Plus	4.25
Jim & Judy's DJ Service	3.30

Company Strengths and Weaknesses

Our company's strengths and weaknesses can be identified using the weighting-scoring model.

Our strengths are as follows:

- Marketing experience.
- DJ operations experience.
- Financial and technical experience.

High confidence is evidenced in core DJ experience and marketing experience. It is important to utilize these key skill sets to gain and maintain market share in the region, which in turn will add to the successful number of years in business.

Our weaknesses are as follows:

- Years in business - zero.
- Medium score in entertainment experience.
- Medium score in financial experience.

Secondary Players

DJ entertainers have become popular over the years because they offer an economical alternative to traditional live entertainment. Customer budget and location space constraints often come into play, thereby increasing the attractiveness of DJ services. We, therefore, identify live entertainment, such as bands, as our secondary competition.

We can compete with live entertainment by:

- Offering a competitive price: Charge less.
- Offering interactive show components: Giveaways, contests, etc.
- Offering streamlined persona: Less equipment equals faster setup.

Marketing Strategy and Plan

Market Strategy

TIP

See the section
Overview of Market Strategies in Chapter 2 *for more details about marketing strategies.*

Jim & Judy's DJ Service will embrace a "nicher strategy" as its marketing strategy. This will allow the company to operate in a market segment, which will avoid clashing with larger competitors. The ideal market niche will display the following characteristics:

• Profitable size.
• Growth potential.
• Neglected by major competitors.
• Can be uniquely served by the market nicher.
• Defensible against major competitors.

In order to meet these characteristics and still maintain a profitable size, the ideal region to address is the San Bernardino County, California, market. This is an inland region and is neglected by many of our competitors. Therefore, the region is underserved and will fit the nicher strategy that we will be embracing. We will be successful in this market because we will be:

• Locating in new and underserved markets.
• Specializing geographically.
• Focusing on a specific market segment.
• In a unique location.

Market Segment

Our strategy is to segment our market into two primary categories:

• Geographic: By region.
• Benefits: Customer perception of our service.

As previously mentioned, our target market will be addressed through our niche strategy, which will address the region of San Bernardino County. We will also stress the benefits of our service in advertisements and in our personal selling efforts:

• Price.
• Image and professionalism.
• Quality.

We will address the following market segments, for the most part:

• Weddings.
• Business events.
• School functions.
• Private parties.

The Marketing Mix

We will utilize a marketing mix in order to:

• Define the service.
• Reach specific market segments through the appropriate distribution channels.
• Price the service.
• Successfully promote the service.

The Service

We will position our service around our central positioning theme:

The Complete Entertainment Solution.

Product Positioning Model

Four scenarios follow and include the elements of price and quality:

PRODUCT POSITION	PRICE	QUALITY
Rip-off	High	Low
Discount	Low	Low
Prestige	High	High
High-value	Low	High

Download the equipment schedule, which is in a Microsoft Excel spreadsheet, from the Web site.

We have determined that high-value positioning is the best way to address the needs of our customers in our target market segments.

Our primary service will be DJ entertainment services that will consist of playing music CDs over a loudspeaker system. We will augment this service with lighting, announcement, and contest services.

We plan to offer an extensive music selection to our clients. This is evidenced by our commitment to $3,000 in program material on the equipment start-up schedule. We believe that music program material is the heart and soul of our operation and is one way that we have chosen to differentiate our service in the marketplace.

The Place

Distribution

We will reach the target market through mobile distribution of our service. We will operate the day-to-day office functions within a home office.

Location

We will concentrate our efforts on clients located in San Bernardino County for the following reasons:

• Location of the clients in reference to the owners' home.
• The chosen market region.
• The underserved attributes of the market.

Pricing Strategy

We surveyed competitor prices for the development of our sales forecast. Our pricing goal is to offer a service that addresses each customer's perception of value. For example, for the city of Ontario, which has a large Latin population, we have decided to institute an *odd* pricing scheme because this population is generally price-sensitive. Therefore, we will price our service by reinforcing the perception of value to this demographic segment. We will price a standard 4-hour gig at $399 rather than $400 in order to reinforce price value.

Discounts

We will offer discounts based on coupon specials. However, our revenue projections do not allow for much concession here because of the commodity nature of the pricing in the DJ business. We will need to inflate pricing of our coupons somewhat so that we can maintain our minimum target service fee of $400 per job, and therefore, stay within the parameters of our sales forecast.

Promotion Strategy

Parameters

- The promotion budget will be distinctly limited.

- The marketing philosophy reflected in this plan emphasizes market segmentation and sharply defined target markets, which are available from our customer profile demographics. Scarce marketing promotion resources will only be invested in high-return segments.

- This plan focus is on the introductory phases of initial opening and secures a budget for continued promotion within these segments.

During the start-up phase of the business, the goal will be to build service identity. This will concentrate around the initial service rollout. The objectives will be:

- Build awareness of our service.
- Present and enhance image of our service.
- Point out a need and create a desire for our service.

The promotion will explain what the service is, what our service has to offer, why we are in business, where we are located, when people can obtain our services, and how people can reach the business.

We will be using pull strategy in order to obtain client awareness of our service. Advertising will be the primary vehicle used to accomplish this goal.

Media Planning

To date, local advertisers have been contacted and are assisting with marketing ideas. We have established an initial rollout budget of $1,000 with a monthly ad budget of $200 to spread across different media:

- Local penny saver.
- Local newspaper - schools.
- Flyers/coupons.
- Co-op advertising.
- Promotional events.

Promotional Budget and Creative Planning

Ad design will be targeted at each demographic segment. Most advertisers will create an ad as part of their overall package. A sketch and logo artwork will be supplied for their use in designing and distributing the ad.

The following chart outlines our advertising/promotion budget.

Media Promotional Budget ($)

Media	1 X Cost	Weekly	Monthly
Brochures	700		
Campus news			75
Direct Mail		15	45
Co-op ads			60
Table tents	300		
Coupons			20
News Publicity			
Total Costs	**1000**	**15**	**200**

We have designed a four-color full-page brochure. The cost of this is $700 for 2,500 pieces. The brochures will be our primary marketing tool. We also ordered 2,500 table tents, which will be distributed on table tops at gigs.

Co-op ads are exchanges and trade-outs with local merchants. We will distribute their coupons if they distribute ours. We will also cooperate with in-group advertising efforts whereby we will share ad space with other local businesses that complement our products. We have budgeted

$60 per month for co-op advertising.

We have budgeted $75 per month for ad space in the local college and high school newspapers.

Publicity is basically *free* advertising. We will provide articles about DJ-related topics to the news media for publication in their newsletters and/or newspapers. Because publicity has an estimated value, it will be an important component to our promotional campaign.

Creative planning and production costs are included in the budget. Judy Johnson, who is a proficient artist, will develop all artwork for the flyers and coupons via computer. Most advertisers will create an ad as part of their overall package. We will ask for a discount for supplied artwork.

Organizational Plan

Owner/Managers

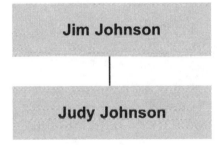

Consultant

CBM Payroll Services:

CBM Payroll Systems will consult with us regarding financial issues and assist with our computer bookkeeping system, which we will manage ourselves.

Manuals and Procedures

We plan to operate our business by ourselves. However, as we operate the business we plan to write a personnel manual, which will establish policy and general guidelines for all employees. Also, we are in the process of writing an operations manual in order to establish basic procedures. This manual will serve as a training tool and serve as a continual reference, which will address government requirements regarding:

• Hazard awareness.
• Fire safety.
• Illness and injury prevention.
• OSHA (Occupational Safety and Health Administration) requirements.

Capital Equipment Budget

We estimate that equipment will cost $9,765. This figure includes sound, lighting, program material, and office equipment.

EQUIPMENT LIST SUMMARY ($)	
DJ sound equipment	3,200
Lighting equipment	620
Program material (music)	3,000
Office equipment	2,145
TOTAL EQUIPMENT	**$9,765**

Financial Projections

Overview

Projections have been prepared as evidenced by the following schedules. We have prepared a complete set of financials for year 1, year 2 and year 3:

• Sales Forecast.
• Pro Forma Income Statement.
• Pro Forma Balance Sheet.
• Cash Flow Statements.

We have $9,000 from savings to invest in this venture, and we have secured a loan of $5,000. This amount is enough to cover all start-up costs.

Income statements serve as operating statements. These give an overview of all revenue and expenses. They also serve as a labor budget and total operating budget for this start-up venture. Refer to the schedule on page 5.6, *Summary Figures,* for the following discussion.

We anticipate low revenue for the first month of operation. However, we anticipate revenue to pick up as we secure contracts with booking agents.

NIAT figure accrues on the Pro Forma Balance Sheet in the cash line item. If possible, we expect to pay off the capital loan of $5,000, in year 2; however, the financial statements currently reflect a loan payment schedule for this amount through year 3. This interest amount is considered in the expense section of our Profit and Loss Statement and the principle amount is denoted on the Balance Sheet.

We will build a substantial equity position of $50,020 at the end of the first year. This figure jumps to $97,020 by the end of the second and third years. These figures represent accruals of revenue and are here primarily for illustration. We will likely draw a salary, which will change these figures.

Our figures represent a positive outlook for our operation. We believe that this will put us in a good position to invest accumulated profits and equity into other operations in the future.

START-UP COST SCHEDULE ($)

Equipment	9,765
Licenses and tax deposits	200
Phone and utility deposit	300
Insurance	600
Advertising	1,000
Miscellaneous	300
TOTAL COSTS	**$12,365**

Summary and Conclusions

The DJ entertainment business is poised for sustained growth. We see a solid growth trend in this area for many years. This growth potential is the essence of this plan because it secures a revenue base from which to operate and secures profit returns for the future.

The owners will commit $9,000 and an additional $5,000 in loans to the fruition of this venture. The strong equity position of this endeavor secures a solid base for operations and provides a sound financial foundation for the future.

The validity of this business concept as exemplified in this plan illustrates a strong potential for success. The plan communicates leadership ability by its operators as evidenced by their business and educational experience. The plan's strong marketing analysis and financial features further identify the operators' business and technical abilities.

Equipment

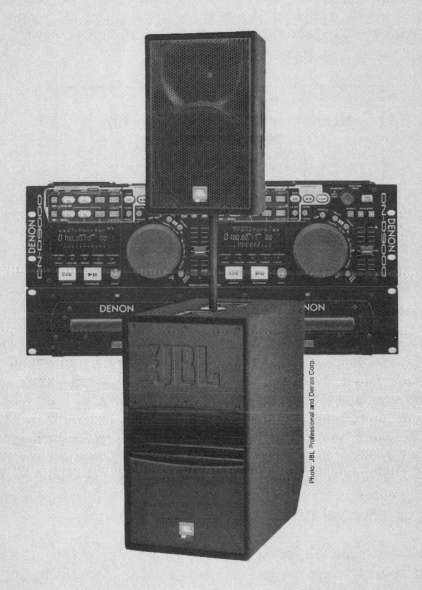

Photo: JBL Professional and Deron Corp.

T his chapter provides practical tips for selecting the right equipment for the job, explaining its function and optimum setup. From the AC power source to the power amps, veteran sound engineer, Tony Crabtree, offers tips and suggestions on how to operate your sound system.

AC Power

We assume that when we plug an appliance in it will work. It usually does and we calmly go on without even considering what has just happened. It works. We got our AC power (Alternating Current). We don't even think about it. However, we cannot assume that all AC power is the same or that it is wired correctly at the wall.

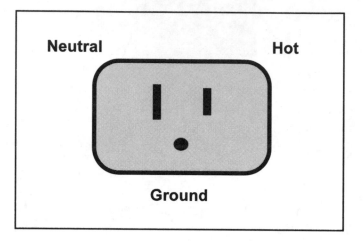

A typical AC outlet is keyed, meaning that you can insert a keyed plug into the receptacle only one way. In the figure above, the neutral receptacle, on the left, is longer than the hot receptacle, on the right. The round ground receptacle is below. However older equipment, such as guitar amps, do not have keyed receptacles adapted to this feature. Some have a "ground switch" that can tie either the neutral or hot receptacle to ground, creating a random hot chassis. This can be very dangerous and can shock a person. Therefore, it is important to have a qualified technician rewire all older equipment to a keyed format, making sure to disable or remove any ground switches that can create a dangerous situation.

A good way to test the integrity of the power at any event is to use a simple AC tester. You can buy these devices for under $20 at any Radio Shack store. Plug the device into any AC receptacle, and it will tell you if it is wired correctly. Buy it and use it. It may save your life one day.

AC Power Conditioning and Regulation

The equipment used in your setup is designed to run at 115 volts 60 Hz (cycles). This voltage would remain constant in a perfect world. The reality is spikes, sags, surges, brownouts, and EMI/RFI are typical anomalies found in today's power lines that could potentially cause problems with audio equipment.

Spikes and surges refer to voltages that are above the normal operating voltage. A spike is a short pulse of energy with voltage as high as 6,000 and lasts for only a few milliseconds. A nearby lightning strike is the most common source of spikes. This much voltage, although brief, is more than enough to cause damage to sensitive electronics and loss of data in digital equipment. Compared to a spike, a voltage surge is a less intense but longer-lasting event. Surges are 10-35% increases in voltage that last from about 15 milliseconds to several minutes. Surges are typical when using power from a generator or when there is a short or open circuit somewhere in the power line.

Sags and brownouts are the complete opposites of spikes and surges. They are voltage drops lasting from a few milliseconds, in the case of sags, to a several minutes or even hours in the case of brownouts. Sags are typically caused by turning on a nearby piece of equipment such as a power amplifier or air conditioner. Brownouts typically occur when the city's power grid is overtaxed, such as during unusually hot or cold weather.

EMI and RFI, or Electromagnetic Interference and Radio Frequency Interference are not damaging to electronic equipment because they are much lower in voltage than spikes or surges, but they can certainly ruin a live show or recording. Nothing is more annoying than a hum or buzz in the sound system.

Power conditioning simply refers to devices designed to *protect* against brief anomalies such as spikes and surges in AC power lines. Conditioning also refers to devices and circuits designed to filter or block out EMI and RFI interference problems.

On the other hand, power regulation refers to devices designed to *correct* fluctuations in voltage such as might occur during a brownout.

The Human Ear

What tool does every engineer and stage performer possess without which the show does not go on? Or, if this tool is damaged in some way beyond repair the show does not go on? Give up? It is your ears.

The human ear is your most precious tool. Protect it and do not abuse it because this tool must last you a lifetime. The amazing human ear is a very complex system. Let's take a look at the basics of how permanent damage to the ear occurs, and how sound engineers and DJs can protect their hearing without compromising the quality of their work.

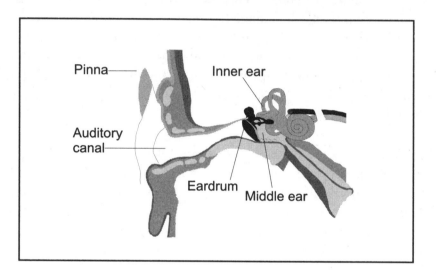

The ear has three basic sections: the outer ear, the middle ear, and the inner ear. The outer ear consists of the the pinna, the auditory canal, and the eardrum. The pinna is the visible part of the ear. It basically captures the sound and directs it into the ear canal where it hits the eardrum. The size and shape of the pinna actually affects how well we hear sounds. This is one reason each person has a slightly different opinion on what sounds good. One person may perceive midrange frequencies a little better than another person who hears the same sound, but perceives the high frequencies a little better because of the way their ears are shaped.

The middle ear then transfers the sound vibrations to the fluid of the inner ear via the three tiny bones we learned about in grammar school: the hammer, the anvil, and the stirrup. Once the sound vibrations enter the inner ear, which is filled with fluid, thousands of tiny hair-like neurons called stereocilia receive the vibrations. The stereocilia transfer this information to our brain, telling us there is a sound.

Imagine that each stereocilia receives only one specific frequency and transfers that specific frequency information to the brain. Now let's imagine that one or a group of stereocilia is constantly exposed to high levels of sound around 5 kilohertz. After awhile, these particular stereocilia become fatigued and if not given a chance to recover will cease to function. Once even a small amount of damage occurs to a specific stereocilia, just like other damaged nerve endings in the body, it will never re-grow. This is why some people lose their hearing at specific frequencies and not at other frequencies.

There are two basic ways we can prevent permanent hearing damage: one, by simply not exposing ourselves to high sound pressure levels such as loud DJ shows, rock shows or loud walkman headphones, and two, by wearing adequate hearing protection devices. According to OSHA (Occupational Health and Safety Administration), we can be exposed to some sound levels for a period of time without suffering permanent loss: 85dB (the sound of heavy traffic) for up to 16 hours per day; 90dB (the sound of loud classical music) for up to 8 hours per day, and 100dB (the sound of a quiet rock-n-roll concert or loud walkman headphones) for less than 2 hours per day. Longer exposure times than these may result in permanent hearing damage.

Ear plugs are an effective means to protect your ears, but perhaps as a musician or DJ you don't like the muffled sound created by most earplugs. Audiologists offer high-fidelity earplugs called the ER-15 and ER-30 that allow a person to still hear detail and clarity in music. They are custom molded to the ear and cost about $125. This price is well worth it. Your ears are precious. Protect them and you will still be able to enjoy music when you are older.

Sound Systems

• Microphones.
• Mixers and turntables.
• Amplifiers.
• Speakers.
• Cables.

Microphones

Dynamic Microphones

Searching for the right microphone for your particular job can often be frustrating. The selection of a mic and also the mic placement can have a huge impact on the sound quality of your sound system.

There are several objectives of microphone selection and placement techniques: First and foremost we are trying to maximize the pickup of the desired sound of an instrument or vocal. Desired sound means either the natural sound of the instrument or some particular sound quality which is appropriate for the application. Second, we want to minimize the pickup of unwanted sound from other instruments or background noise. Lastly, to maximize gain-before-feedback. Obtaining the right microphone will most likely require a little give and take from each of these objectives.

Dynamic and condenser mics are the two most commonly used microphone types in live-sound reinforcement. The operating principle of the microphone determines some of the basic capabilities of the microphone.

Elements of a Dynamic Mic

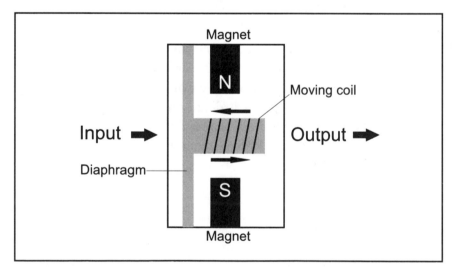

Dynamic mics operate similar to the voice coil of a loudspeaker, only in reverse. Sound waves strike the diaphragm, which then vibrates. This vibration then moves a small coil of wire within a magnetic field. It is this motion within the magnetic field that generates the electrical voltage that we know as the audio signal. Dynamic mics are generally very economical, very rugged, and can provide excellent sound quality. They can handle extremely high sound pressure levels: it is almost impossible to overload a dynamic mic. Also, they are relatively unaffected by extremes of temperature and humidity. Dynamics are probably the most widely used microphones in general sound reinforcement. Good examples of a dynamic microphone that most people are familiar with are the Shure SM57 and the SM58.

Condenser Microphones

Let's talk about the operating principal of condenser microphones. They are based on an electrically-charged diaphragm and backplate assembly. Here, sound waves vibrate a very thin metal diaphragm. The diaphragm is mounted just in front of a rigid metal backplate. In electrical terms, this assembly is known as a capacitor (which in the old days was referred to as a condenser). A capacitor has the ability to store a charge or voltage. When the element is charged an electric field is created between the diaphragm and the backplate, proportional to the spacing between them. It is the variation of this spacing, due to the motion of the diaphragm as it is struck by sound waves, that produces the electrical voltage we know as the audio signal.

Elements of a Condenser Mic

Because the electrical voltage of the condenser element is very, very low, all condenser microphones have a built-in mic preamp to boost the voltage to a normal operating level. This active circuitry requires that all condenser mics be powered either by a battery or by phantom power.

Phantom power is a method of supplying power to the mic through the microphone cable itself.

Generally, condenser mics are more expensive than dynamics and are less rugged. Also, extremes of temperature and humidity can adversely affect a condenser. In spite of these drawbacks condensers can be readily made with higher sensitivity and can provide a smoother, more natural sound, especially at higher frequencies. Flat frequency response and extended frequency range are much easier to obtain in a condenser. Finally, a condenser mic can be made very small without significant loss of performance.

Microphone Polar Patterns

Directionality is what determines how sensitive a microphone is to sound relative to the direction or angle from which the sound arrives. The most common directional types of microphones in live sound are omni-directional and uni-directional. These are typically plotted in a polar pattern on paper to graphically display the mic's directionality. The polar pattern shows the variation in sensitivity 360 degrees around the mic.

The omni-directional mic has equal sensitivity at all angles. It's pick up pattern is a full 360 degrees. An omni-directional mic will pick up the most ambient noise compared with other pickup patterns. An omni should be placed as close as possible to the sound source to overcome any ambient noise. The main drawback of an omni-directional mic is that it cannot be aimed away from speakers because it may cause feedback. There are not many examples of omni microphones used in live music. However, a common use is for a lectern/podium mic or for a lapel or lavalier mic.

The unidirectional mic is most sensitive to sound coming from one direction: the front. There are variations of unidirectional mics, the most common being the cardioid. It gets this name because its polar pattern is heart-shaped. A cardioid mic is least sensitive 180° off axis and thus provides the most rejection to feedback directly behind the mic. A unidirectional mic is great for providing isolation from both unwanted off-axis sound and from ambient stage noise.

Microphone Polar Patterns

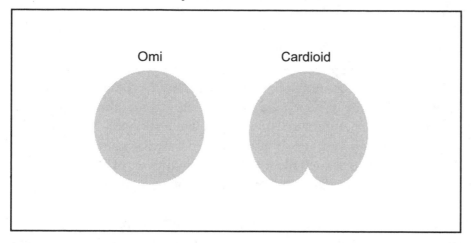

Omi   Cardioid

Variations of the unidirectional pickup pattern are supercardioid and hypercardioid. While a cardioid maintains its highest amount of rejection 180° off-axis, super- and hyper-cardioid mics provide extreme rejection about 120° off-axis, behind and slightly to either side of the mic. When placed properly they can provide more focused pickup and less ambient noise than the cardioid pattern, but they have some pickup directly at the rear, called a rear lobe.

Wireless Microphone Systems

Many DJs are using wireless technology as it becomes more and more affordable. In live sound, its most common applications are wireless microphones, wireless musical instrument rigs, and wireless in-ear monitor systems. There are several different types of wireless systems available, the main distinctions being UHF (Ultra High Frequency) or VHF (Very High Frequency) and diversity or non-diversity. The term "diversity" is a common source of confusion for many people. What is diversity, are there different types and which one is best?

First, let's dispel the most common misconception: diversity does not refer to using two or more frequencies. Each transmitter emits only one RF (Radio Frequency) signal at a specific frequency at any one time. This is true even in the case of synthesized transmitters capable of switching between several different frequencies.

These transmitters can only operate on one frequency at a time. The receiver is also tuned to this same frequency, and if the receiver is of high quality, it rejects all other RF signals except for one the transmitter is sending out.

So if diversity doesn't deal with multiple frequencies, what is it? The term diversity as it applies to wireless technology refers to receiving the transmitted signal at more than one antenna. This can be accomplished in different ways, some of which are more effective than others. "True" diversity or "multiple receiver" diversity is unquestionably the most effective method. True diversity uses two separate RF receiver sections each with its own separate antenna. Internal switching or blending circuitry then decides which signal or combination of signals to utilize.

The way in which the different manufacturers utilize multiple-receiver technology varies widely and can greatly affect the usability of a system. Also, there are other less effective methods of diversity such as "antenna" diversity. This is where multiple antennas are used but there is only one receiver section to accept the RF. This is generally considered a substandard diversity system and should be avoided due to its substantial limitations.

DJ Mixing Consoles and Turntables

A major investment for most DJs, purchasing a new mixing console or tuntable requires careful consideration. A series of logical questions is the best method of determining your specific needs. The trick is to ask the right questions. There are many different models and options of mixing consoles available to DJs today just like there are different makes, models, and options of cars.

The first question that most people instinctively ask is: What is the best model? Immediately followed by the inevitable: How much will it cost? or How much can I afford this? Both are very good questions, but how does one decide?

The function of a mixing console is to combine or mix signals. In a traditional DJ setup there are two turntables connected to a mixing console. The primary mixing function is to crossfade between the two.

The best mixing console is one that meets your budget requirements. It must have the necessary headroom gain and crossfade functions to qualify it as a DJ mixer.

Low headroom and noise are a sign of a low-quality mixer. Premature preamp clipping in the mixer can damage your power amp and speakers. Likewise, a cheap mixer can exhibit noise that can be a nuisance in live situations.

Most event DJs use CDs these days. CD players have digital outputs on them that can be connected directly to a digital mixer. This reduces noise because the signal does not have to be converted to a analog signal before it gets to the mixer. Digital mixers are usually more expensive than their analog counterparts. However, they can save you money if you require built-in effects, such as audio delays, compressors, pitch-shifters, etc., because many of these units have the effects built in. Conversely, if you plan to use vinyl as your program material, an analog mixer will work just fine.

Therefore, the format of your music catalog is a primary determining factor when choosing a DJ mixer.

Turntables come in basically two configurations: Analog vinyl or CD. There are many models and that have different price points to choose from. To learn more about what is available visit the Web site where you will find a listing of retail suppliers of these units.

Once you have narrowed your choice of make, model, and options, you are ready to shop around for the best price. Mail-order catalogs may have good prices, but you don't normally have much support after the sale. On the other hand, your local pro-sound shop personnel will usually take the time to answer your questions and help you make an intelligent decision and also be there for you after the sale to help you when you most need it.

Power Amplifiers

Amplifier Selection

Everyone who buys, uses, or designs a sound system inevitably asks the question, "How large an amplifier do I need?" Answers to this question vary widely, and should somehow be related to the loudspeakers the amp will drive. Usually, the answer will be tied to the loudspeaker's power handling capability.

Here are a couple of common misconceptions about choosing a power amp:

- The amplifier power should equal the power-handling rating of the speaker. In other words, a 500-watt speaker would be powered by a 500 Watt amp. Wrong.

- The loudspeaker's power rating should be more than the rated output of the power amp, i.e. underpower the loudspeaker. The intent here is not to overdrive the loudspeaker with more power than it can handle. This is also wrong.

The correct concept is this: The amplifier should be able to produce more power than the speaker's power rating. This eliminates the possibility of a smaller amplifier reaching its maximum output and producing a distorted signal, at which time the speaker could be damaged, even though it was not overdriven.

The AES (Audio Engineering Society) loudspeaker rating method considers the maximum power that a loudspeaker can handle for a period of two hours without failure. It also considers a minimum of 6dB of headroom, which is consistent with the compressed program material commonly reproduced by today's sound systems. Without getting too technical here, 6dB represents a 4 to 1 power ratio. This means that 400 watts is necessary to deliver 100 watts average power to the loudspeaker.

Here are some guidelines for choosing your power amplifier:

- **Determine the AES power rating of the loudspeaker.** This is usually found in the specifications. If not, a close estimate is to use one half of the continuous average power rating of the loudspeaker.

- **Add 6dB of amplifier headroom.** This means that it is necessary to multiply the continuous power rating by a factor of 4 to determine the actual power amplifier size. Up to 10dB of headroom is even better for the loudspeaker because true audio signals often have large peaks that will be less likely to be clipped due to insufficient power.

- **Operate the amplifier at a normal level.** This means that the peak lights should only come on occasionally. This ensures that the average power delivered to the loudspeaker will be well below the maximum available power from the amplifier.

Let's look at an example. We have a speaker with a continuous average power rating of 200 watts. Dividing this by 2 gives us an AES power rating of 100 watts. We then multiply 100 watts times 4 to give us 6dB of headroom. This results in an actual power amplifier size of 400 watts per channel.

Speakers

Impedance Calculations

How many speakers can I plug into a power amp? This is a very important topic when designing any sound system and involves an explanation of the electrical term "impedance". The impedance of a loudspeaker is the total opposition to AC current flow as presented to the output of the power amplifier.

The amount of power extracted from an amplifier by a speaker is directly related to the impedance of the speaker. Loudspeaker specifications will always include a figure called nominal impedance, given in ohms. The lower the impedance, the more power the loudspeaker will draw from the amp. For this reason, most amplifier power ratings are given at two or more load impedances, usually either 4 ohms or 8 ohms, and the 4 ohm power is usually close to twice the 8 ohm power.

The load impedance seen by an amplifier must always be greater than zero. If it were to equal zero, the amplifier output would be short circuited and the resulting infinite current demand would seriously damage the power amp.

Practically speaking, the load impedance on an amplifier channel should never be less than 4 ohms. Even though some amplifiers are rated for 2 ohm operation, it is not advisable to load an amplifier this heavily in professional use. Not only will the amplifier be stressed, potentially causing it to overheat and shutdown, but you will have to use an extremely large loudspeaker cable to handle the extra current, especially over long runs.

Connecting a single speaker to an amplifier output is a simple matter, but what happens to the impedance load when two or more loudspeakers are connected to that output? There are two basic ways to connect multiple loudspeakers to a single output: in series or in parallel.

When speakers are connected in series, the current from the amplifier passes through one speaker before it passes through the next and so on. In this method, the impedances of the speakers is added together to find the total impedance load of the amplifier. For example two 8-ohm speakers connected in series would have a total impedance of 16 ohms. There are two main disadvantages of series connections: One, the result is a higher impedance load and therefore less power is extracted from the amplifier. Two, if one speaker fails, the entire connection is broken and all the loudspeakers will cease to function.

Series Speaker Connections

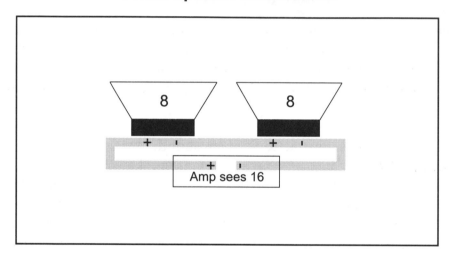

When speakers are connected in parallel, the total impedance load is a bit more complicated to calculate. Luckily though, in the special case where all speakers are the same nominal impedance we can calculate their impedance very easily. If two speakers are connected in parallel with the same impedance, then the total impedance load is exactly half of either one. In other words, two 8-ohm speakers connected in parallel would have a total impedance of 4 ohms. The main advantage of parallel connections is if one speaker fails, the other will continue to work. Parallel connections are by far the most widely used in professional sound systems.

Parallel Speaker Connections

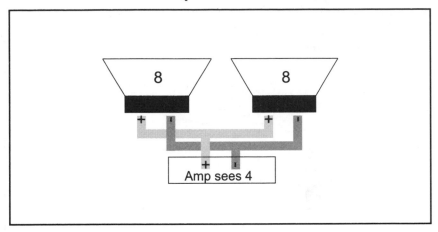

The number of speakers that can be connected to a power amp is dependent upon the impedance load of all the speakers not the power ratings of the amplifier or the speakers.

Adding a Subwoofer

Adding a subwoofer to your sound system is a simple way to increase its performance and add that extra "punch". Bi-amplified or tri-amplified systems offer a number of performance advantages over conventional systems.

In order to bi-amp a system, a passive or active crossover network is required to divide up the total frequency range. Passive crossovers are located after the power amp and are usually built into the speaker enclosure. Active crossovers are designed to be inserted into the signal chain before the power amp. Since the total frequency range is divided up before the power amplifier, separate amplifier channels are required for each frequency range. Thus, a two-way bi-amplified system would have an amplifier channel for the high frequencies and a second channel for the low frequencies.

A Bi-amplified System

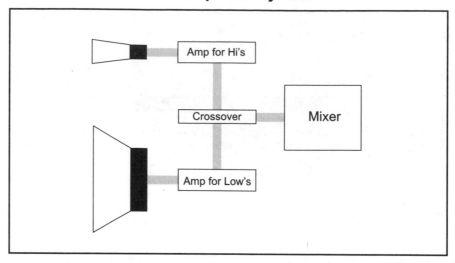

Some systems combine active crossovers with passive crossovers. For example, a three-way sound system may utilize an active crossover to split the lowest from the mid and high frequencies, feeding each band to a separate power amplifier. The high-frequency amplifier's output is then fed to a passive crossover, whose output then goes to the mid-frequency and high-frequency drivers. Such a system is said to be bi-amplified but is actually a three-way system.

A traditional passive crossover is made up of capacitors, inductors, and resistors. These components use up some power. Bi-amplifying the system with an active crossover removes these losses, thus improving the sound system's efficiency. In other words, more sound level for a given amount of power amplifier output.

Increased headroom is also gained because in musical material, most of the energy is in the low frequencies, with very little in the high range. When both high and low frequencies are present in a signal, the stronger low frequencies can use up amplifier power, leaving little or no reserve for the highs so they are more apt to cause the power amplifier to clip. In a bi-amplified system a smaller amp can handle the high frequencies and a second amp can handle the low frequencies, thus less overall amplifier power is needed.

The increased clarity and punch gained from using a bi-amped system with a subwoofer is well worth the extra expense of the active crossover and extra amplifier. Ask your local pro-sound shop about what is right for you.

Cables

Balanced vs. Unbalanced Cables

A live show can have hundreds of feet of cable running all over place. When making cable runs of any length it's important to be able to reject any noise that may jump on the line from a number of sources. Radio Frequency or RF, noise from dimmers or fluorescent lighting, CB radio transmissions, AM/FM radio transmissions, and more can end up hitch-hiking along with your signal. Think about it, when you lay out a length of cable you are essentially making an antenna. When you lay out thousands of feet of antennas it can be a nightmare.

The best way to remedy this is to use balanced connections. The difference between balanced and unbalanced cable is an extra conductor in the wire. An unbalanced connection runs two conductors, a positive (+) hot and a ground. A balanced connection runs three conductors, a positive (+) hot, a negative (-) cold, and a ground. What makes the difference is not in the cable but in what happens at either end, before and after the signal travels down the cable. Any cable can be an antenna and a noise collector.

Unbalanced TRS Cable Configuration

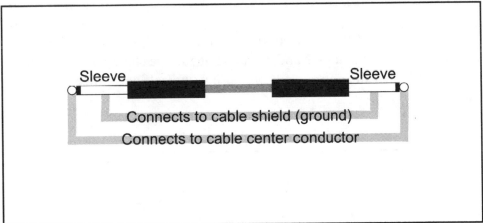

Sleeve   Sleeve
Connects to cable shield (ground)
Connects to cable center conductor

High impedance lines use unbalanced circuits where one signal lead flows through the center of the cable and is surrounded by a shield that is grounded. This shield is also used as the second signal lead, as illustrated in the figure above.

Let's look at balanced connectors. There are two common types, one is an XLR or cannon plug and the other is a Tip-Ring-Sleeve (TRS) ¼-inch connector. The interesting thing that balanced connections does has to do with tricking the noise on the line into phase canceling itself out of existence. Here's how it happens. A balanced connection first runs through a differential amplifier which splits the hot signal into two and flips one half 180 degrees out of phase. This travels along the cable as plus and minus along with the ground on three separate conductors. Along the way the usual noise is encountered and picked up by the line.

Balanced TRS Cable Configuration

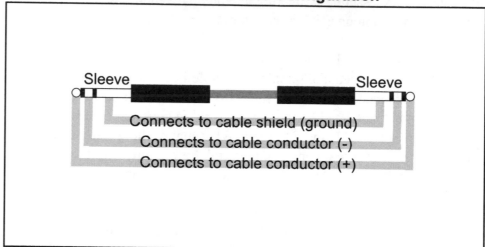

Sleeve   Sleeve

Connects to cable shield (ground)
Connects to cable conductor (-)
Connects to cable conductor (+)

At the other end of the connection, the minus is flipped back into phase and you end up with a plus and a ground again, the same as when you started. But now the noise is out of phase with itself and cancels completely.

XLR Connector Pin Configuration

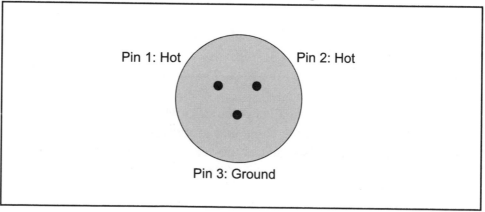

Pin 1: Hot   Pin 2: Hot

Pin 3: Ground

So now you can make long cable runs and not worry about errant noise entering the picture. All pro sound systems are balanced all the way from the microphones and direct boxes through the snake and to the house and monitor consoles, and even to the outboard gear. Buying balanced gear is a bit more expensive but pays off big time in the sound and noise department.

Three-pin XLR connectors are not always wired the same way. This can create a problem because either pin 1 or pin 3 can be the ground. A typical XLR connector pin configuration is illustrated on the previous page. One way to remedy a pin configuration mismatch is to keep adapters available that will convert from one pin to another.

Cable Maintenance

Everyone involved with live sound has heard the results of a bad cable at one point or another. There is nothing worse than snap, crackle, and pop at 90 decibels. A single bad cable can cripple an entire sound system (and the show) if you don't happen to have a replacement handy or have the skills to repair it. The most expensive equipment is only as good as the cable that connects it.

Preventive maintenance is the best way to avoid that embarrassing snap, crackle, and pop. Don't wait until you're setting up for the show to find out that you have a bad cable somewhere in the system. Test the cables at home or in your workshop with a good quality cable tester periodically. A cable tester is a small box-like device that has a variety of connector types such as XLR for microphone cable, ¼-inch or speak-on for speaker cable, and RCA for line level cables. Both male and female connectors are provided to create a loop out of the tester and then back into the tester. When a cable is connected in this fashion, the tester will indicate short circuits or open circuits and will usually specify which conductor within the cable is faulty. When testing, be sure to give the cable a good workout by pulling and shaking it vigorously to expose any intermittent problems.

Also check your cables periodically to make sure that all the parts or screws on the connector itself are properly tightened. This makes sure that the strain relief mechanism is properly seated against the cable and is doing its job. When choosing new cables or connectors, choose connectors with good strain relief. Not all connector brands are created equal.

Finally, learn how to coil your cables properly. The proper way involves an over and under method, sometimes known as a "broadcast wrap", which does not introduce any twists into the cable. Careful coiling and storage of your cables will definitely extend their useful life.

Operating a Sound System

Turn On Sequencing in Sound Systems

A potentially damaging pop is caused by transients created when any piece of equipment is turned on or off. In a typical small sound system, most of your equipment's AC power is plugged into a single power strip or power conditioner. When this power source is turned on, all of the equipment including the mixer and the power amp are turned on simultaneously. This means that any transients created by the console are amplified by the power amp and then sent to the loudspeakers. These transients can easily exceed the normal voltage output by the console, creating a clipped signal within the power amp. Repeatedly sending this clipped signal to a loudspeaker can easily damage a voice coil.

The easiest way to avoid these embarrassing and potentially damaging transient pops is to educate the sound system user to use a stepped turn-on sequence and a stepped turn-off sequence.

When turning on the sound system, the console and all signal processing gear such as EQ boxes, limiters, and crossovers, upstream of the power amp should be turned on first. Then, turn on the power amplifier. When turning off the system, simply reverse this order. Turn off the power amp first and then turn off the rest of the signal processing gear and then the console. By making this turn-on and off sequence a habit, you will not only protect your speakers but avoid the embarrassment of those sometimes annoyingly loud pops.

In larger sound systems, there is another reason to use the turn-on sequence. Today's power amps sometimes require the full capacity of a 20-amp circuit to accommodate the large inrush of current required by the amp when it is initially powered up. Once powered the amplifier then operates at a much lower current. When turning on systems with numerous power amps, simply pausing for 3 or 4 seconds before turning on the next amp will avoid tripping a breaker.

Proper Gain Structure

Home stereos and power amps usually have only one master volume control. That's easy to deal with. But when you are faced with that sea of controls on some mixing consoles, you may find multiple knobs or faders that all affect the same output. Mixing consoles also have level meters. Level meters come in many forms, from a simple clip LED up to an analog needle sweeping against a dB scale. They all tell you one important thing, how close you are to distortion. Knowing this fact can keep you from adding noise to your signal path. In addition, a meter can tell you how far away you are from the noise floor of any particular device. We're not only talking about analog devices, but digital devices as well.

There's grunge noise at both ends of either device. Basically it's like this: Add too much gain and you'll overload the input of your device adding nasty distortion. Don't add enough gain and you're residing down near the noise floor of the device. Ideally you want to hover as near as you can to distortion without crossing the line. This gives you the best signal-to-noise ratio. The ideal is to maintain the best signal-to-noise ratio throughout your signal path. That may sound as easy as nearly maxing out all your meters on your various gear, however sometimes there are gain stages that don't have metering or pathways that have multiple gain stages. For instance, your mic pre-gain feeds the fader which is another gain stage, which feeds the subgroup fader which is yet another gain stage! That's three chances to add noise before you even get to the main output.

Managing all these different gain stages and maintaining adequate signal-to-noise ratios is key to having a good-sounding sound system. When you are mixing, having gain stages within the console working efficiently with each other and with other gain stages outside the console should be your main focus.

Many mixers provide meters for monitoring output levels, but often do not provide clipping indicators. In contrast, most signal processors, such as EQ boxes or power amps provide clipping indicators but do not provide meters. The two can be used together to provide better gain structure management for the entire sound system.

To achieve optimum signal-to-noise ratio, sound equipment should be operated so the program peaks are close to the maximum output level of the device. One solution is to increase the output level of the mixer until the clipping indicator on the next device (usually the equalizer) comes on. At that point the equalizer has been maxed out and the signal level from the mixer should not be increased further. A procedure similar to this should then be performed on the next device in the signal chain, such as a limiter or crossover. This time the input level control should be increased until the clipping indicator comes on. In this manner, each device in the signal chain is operating well above its noise floor and each should reach clipping at about the same time. Make a note of this operating level as indicated on the main meter of your mixing console and mark it.

Power Amplifier Gain

A common misconception about the knob on a power amplifier is that it controls the number of watts available from the amplifier. This would explain why this knob is often set wide open. Most engineers would not want to reduce the power output capability of their amp. However, this knob is not a watt knob!

Then what does this level control do? It adjusts the input sensitivity of the amplifier. Imagine that there are two separate stages inside the power amplifier. One is called the input and one is called the output. The output stage is the stage that actually provides the "watts" or amplified audio to your speakers. The full capability of the output stage is always available. On most amps the output stage only needs one or two volts from the input stage to drive it to its full power rating. More than one or two volts would drive this output stage into clipping and that's when bad things start to happen such as distortion and blown speaker components.

Let's back up a step and talk about the other devices in the signal chain before the amplifier. Most mixers, EQ boxes, and crossovers have output voltages in the 8-10 volt range when operated near clipping or in their 0dB range, which is recommended.

So now how do we reduce this 8-10 volts from the EQ to the 1-2 volts that the output stage of the power amp likes to see? Remember, more than one or two volts will cause the amp to clip and damage your speakers. This is where the input level control of the amplifier comes in handy. By using this knob to attenuate the audio signal at the input stage of the power amplifier, we can give the output stage the exact amount of voltage needed to reach its full power output without clipping.

Gain overlap at the front end of the power amp is what allows us to operate other devices well above their noise floor. Otherwise, in order to keep the amp from clipping, we would have to operate the mixer and EQ at a much lower level.

The Sound Check

The sound check is simply a series of tests to make sure everything is operating properly. There are a lot of things in a sound system to set up, and it is very easy to make a mistake somewhere along the way. Running these simple tests will make it easier to quickly find and isolate these mistakes without unnecessary aggravation. At first, it may look a little complicated, but once you get the hang of it you should be able to go through all the testing procedures in just a very few minutes.

To begin testing, it is a good idea to *zero* the board by setting all the knobs and faders to relatively neutral positions. To do this, turn all the mic pre-gains on the individual channels all the way down, set all of the EQ knobs on the input channels (Low, Mid, High) to the straight up twelve o'clock position; turn all the effects and auxiliary knobs all the way down, and set all the "pan" (balance) knobs to twelve o'clock. Finally make sure the main and monitor master levels are all the way down.

- **Step 1: Set normal settings.** Gradually turn the main (Volume or Level) knob or slider up to near its normal setting. On knobs, straight up at twelve o'clock is good. On sliders, three quarters of the way up is good. These settings will vary depending on the mixing console and the personal preferences of the DJ.

- **Step 2: Audio check.** While playing a song, gradually turn up the "level" knob or slider for that input channel until you can clearly hear the song coming out of the speakers. If you don't hear the song, recheck your connections and knob settings.

- **Step 3: Listen to setup.** Have someone else run the system while you go out to the speakers and listen to them to see if each is working. Make sure to place your head in front of the midrange horns and the individual speakers in each cabinet to check them individually. If a whole cabinet is not working, check your connections to that cabinet. If just a speaker or horn within a cabinet isn't working, check to make sure you plugged the cord into the "full range" input on the speaker. If it still isn't working, you probably have a bad internal connection inside the speaker cabinet or a blown speaker or horn.

Proper Equalization (EQ)

Equalization is probably one of the most misused tools in live sound. The first ingredient in knowing how to equalize is knowing what to equalize. If you have quality equipment, very little (if any) EQ should be required.

Use a minimal amount of EQ on the input channels of your console and use the correct EQ for your vocal microphone. Use low frequency roll-off for vocals. Avoid pumping the bass. It can make your sound system sound like mud!

There are as many opinions on how to use EQ in live audio as there are live sound engineers. Some engineers prefer to use EQ to "flavor" their sound, others use it solely as a corrective device to control feedback. Take the time to practice and experiment with an equalizer. Learn how an EQ actually affects a particular sound. Then trust your ears to tell you what and how much EQ you really need.

Outboard Audio Processing Equipment

The term outboard means using processing effects that are not contained inside the mixing console, but rather are separate products that are used to alter the sound in some way.

Compressors

Q: How do I set a compressor to work well with live vocals?

Working with compressors in live sound is not difficult and can really add that polished touch to your live mixes. Have you ever been in a situation with a vocalist who was so dynamic that his or her loudest notes caused distortion in the sound system, yet when you turned the person's channel gain down low enough to avoid distortion, you could hardly hear the soft notes?

This situation is very common and is easily dealt with through the use of a compressor. Compressors are signal processors that reduce the dynamic range of an input signal by allowing only a small increase in output level for any signal exceeding a certain threshold. Most compressors have six controls: input gain, threshold, compression ratio, attack time, release time, and output gain.

When setting up your compressor for vocals:

• **Step 1: Adjust the input level** so the input is well above the noise floor but does not clip the input stage.

• **Step 2: Choose an appropriate compression ratio** for vocals; 2.5:1 is usually a good starting point, but never go higher than 3:1; this amount of compression could sound very unnatural. Setting the threshold is the next crucial step. Compression should only occur on the loudest portions of the song, therefore the threshold should be set so that only the loudest notes exceed the threshold point, leaving the quiet notes unprocessed.

Compressors for vocals are typically connected to the mixer through a patch point known as an "insert". This insert jack provides a convenient way of inserting the compressor into the vocalist's input channel, typically after the mic pre-amp and before the channel EQ. In this manner you can precisely control the vocalist's dynamic range.

Another typical method is to insert the compressor into a subgroup channel containing a submix of all the vocalists in the group. If you are on a budget and cannot afford a separate compressor for each vocalist, this method is a great compromise. It will reduce the overall dynamics of the vocalists and allow you keep the vocal mix upfront without overloading the system on peaks.

The compression ratio is simply the ratio of the amount of change in output level (in dB) to the amount of change in input level (in dB). For example, let's suppose we have a 2:1 compression ratio. Any sound exceeding the set threshold by 16 dB will be reduced by a factor of 2 resulting in only an 8dB increase in sound above the set threshold. If the compression ratio were set at 4:1, then this same 16dB change in sound above the threshold would be reduced to only 4dB of change above the threshold.

The attack time is the speed at which the signal is reduced after it reaches the threshold. And similarly, the release time is the speed at which the signal is restored to its original value once it decreases back below the threshold.

There is no one attack or release value that is appropriate for all situations. Too fast an attack time causes unnatural program level changes and a lot of distortion of the low-frequency signals as the compressor tries to react to every little change in the input level. If the attack time is too slow then the compressor may not react at all to quick transients such as a hit on a tambourine. Also, too fast a release time results in what is known as pumping or breathing as the gain changes too fast. Yet on the other hand, too slow a release time causes the quieter portions of the audio to be lost while the gain is still reduced due to the louder, longer input signals.

Many models of compressors feature automatic attack and release controls. Professionals recommend using this automatic feature because misadjusting these controls can cause major problems in the sound.

Compression ratios and attack or release settings for typical applications are generally agreed upon by most engineers. For vocals, a good setting ranges between 2.5:1 and 3:1 with a moderately fast attack and a fast release time because there are very few low frequencies in vocals and many quick transients from consonants.

Limiters

Q: How do I set a limiter to protect my speakers?

In live sound, a limiter can be used to protect speakers from mechanical destruction in the event of a dropped microphone for example. They do this by limiting the peak level that will be fed to the amplifiers and speakers.

There is some misconception that compressors and limiters are two different devices. Because their circuitry is almost identical, the real distinction between a compressor and limiter is how the device is used. Compressors are used to reduce the dynamic range of an input signal by allowing only a small increase in output level for any signal exceeding a certain threshold. A limiter on the other hand is used to restrict the dynamic range of an input signal by allowing no increase in output level for any signal exceeding a certain threshold level.

Limiters for speaker protection are typically inserted into the signal chain as the last device before the power amplifier. In setting up your compressor/limiter for speaker protection:

• **Step 1: Adjust the input level** so the input is well above the noise floor but does not clip the input stage.

• **Step 2: Choose an appropriate compression ratio for limiting**; anything above 10:1 is considered to be appropriate for limiting. Setting the threshold is the next crucial step. Limiting should only occur on the loudest peaks of the music, therefore the threshold should be set so that only the loudest signals exceed the threshold point, leaving the quieter portions of the music unprocessed. This threshold setting is very important because if it is too low you will get way too much compression and your music will sound very unnatural.

• **Step 3: Apply typical program material** by listening to the output as you adjust the attack. For limiting, use the fastest attack rate available without audible distortion. Then set the decay time slow enough that you don't hear excessive pumping or breathing, yet fast enough that the program is not ducked unnecessarily after a loud passage.

The increased performance of your sound system through limiting is generally perceived as an increase in volume. As you reduce the peaks you are also able to bring the level of the softest passages up. Limiting is also an effective method of protecting your investment in your sound system and is well worth the extra expense. Ask your local pro-sound shop about what models are right for you.

Rack Mounting Your Gear

Choosing the Right Rack

When buying a 19-inch rack, don't just figure out how many spaces your gear will take and then buy that size rack. This is a mistake that will cost you plenty when you quickly outgrow your available rack space. Most people soon wind up with enough gear to fill a 4-foot 19-inch rack or about 26-30 spaces. What is a space? A space equals 1.75 inches.

Choose the right case grade for your application. If you are looking for a rack case for the road, I recommend a shock-mounted case. This is a case within a case. The inner case is a standard 19-inch rack case but it is surrounded by foam, or suspended by springs, from the outer case. This type case can ensure that your gear will work after it has been unloaded; of course it is much more expensive. Companies such as Anvil, Calzone, and others charge between $350 and $600. This may seem expensive but remember no insurance policy can help you replace broken gear immediately on the road so go for the better case. If your gear will stay mostly in your home studio, choose an all-metal rack. There are low-priced units by Hammond and better units by Premier. They can range from $200 to $450. Since they are metal they are better suited for shielding from RF interference.

Look to see that your rack has rear 19-inch rack mounting rails as well. This will enable you to mount other gear, fans, power conditioners, outlet strips, etc. on the rear of the rack.

If you are buying a large 4-foot high rack, keep in mind that wheels are a must! This is true for the road or in the studio. Remember, there will come a time during a session or live gig that you will have to trouble-shoot something behind the rack.

If you are traveling, it is best to use multiple rack systems in order to limit your liability. Splitting up your gear can save the family jewels. For example, playing a gig where staircases are involved is risky. All it takes is one slip and you can loose the equipment in a rack.

Keeping it Cool

The biggest mistake most people make when setting up their rack is putting all the gear in the rack with no thought given to ventilation. Make sure the back of the rack is as open as possible. Leave at least one space between heavy heat-producing gear (power amplifiers). Use fans for better results. If you are on stage and noise is not a problem, have exhaust fans mounted at the top of the rear of your rack. Have them mounted in a standard 19-inch rack panel. Make sure the fans blow the air out of the rack, not into it. For an extra cooling boost, install fans at the bottom of the rack that blow air into the rack. Then close up all the empty spaces on the back of the rack with empty 19-inch rack filler panels. These empty panels come in all sizes from one space to five and seven space sizes. Also close up any open spaces on the front of the rack in order to use this double fan cooling technique.

Use AC Outlet Strips

Install AC outlet strips in your rack so that all the gear can be plugged in ready to go. Look for an outlet strip that has a circuit breaker to protect your gear. Most outlet strips have 15-amp breakers. If your power amplifier load exceeds 15 amps, use enough outlet strips to cover the load.

To calculate the number of amps needed by your equipment, simply add up the current ratings of your equipment. This information is available on the back badge of the equipment or in the manual.

Power Conditioners and Power Stabilizers

Another elaborate but well worth it investment is adding a power conditioner to your rack. They are sold by the number of amps that they are rated. Power conditioners can quiet noisy AC lines in most situations although they are not a cure-all. If you play in clubs, large halls, and large auditoriums, power conditioners can prevent power spikes and transients from damaging your gear. Many memory banks of synthesizer patches have been lost to a lightning storm while on stage. There are more expensive power stabilizers that will keep the voltage at a desired 115 or 120 volts even during a brownout where the voltage can drop to 25 volts. This will ensure that you will not have to reload your samples on stage in the middle of the show. Usually your power conditioner will be mounted on the rear of your rack at or near the bottom.

TIP
See page 6.3 for more about power conditioning and power regulation.

Building Your Own Connector Panel

One way to make connecting your gear a snap is installing a connector panel on the rear of your rack. Buy a 5-or-7 space blank 19-inch panel. Install a balanced male cannon connector for each output and a few extras as spares on the panel. To solve difficult grounding schemes install a single throw single pole mini-bat toggle switch above each male cannon connector. Wire the switch to intercept pin 1 on the cannon connector. In this way you can easily lift pin 1 for problem situations. Note: Make sure that each of the connectors pin 1 is not touching the chassis of the metal panel on which they are mounted. This could cause a severe ground loop. Companies such as Conquest Sound make pre-made panels with the connectors all mounted in many different configurations.

Make Your Own Wiring Harness

If you've gone the route above and built a rear connector panel you might want to add multi-pin connectors to your panel as well. A multi-pin DL connector, which comes in male and female chassis mount configurations, can connect the equivalent of 24 cannon connectors. For stage setups the cost of wiring multi-pin connectors is justified by the amount of setup time they save.

Install your DL connectors so that they are wired in parallel with your cannon connector panel. This way you have both and in an emergency there is an alternative way to hook things up.

You can make your own snakes to connect to the DL connectors. Use Connectronics multi-colored snake wire. It comes in 8 shielded pairs in a snake, colored coded for easy hookup. You can use three lengths for each DL connector. Install the opposite sex DL on the rack end and male cannons for the stage end to interface with most stage snake boxes. You can also have each end terminate in an balanced Bantam plug or build another snake for use in the studio. Male balanced Bantam plugs will patch directly into most professional consoles, so you can have the right snake for stage and studio.

Use a Midi (Musical Instrument Digital Interface) Pacthbay

Install a Midi patchbay in your rack. Wire all the ins and outs of all your midi connections to the bay. If you set it up correctly and use good quality Midi cables, you should never have to go behind the rack to swap Midi cables again. This is great for Midi controlled lighting units and Midi controlled mixers.

Live Show Safety

Have you ever been to a live show and noticed a speaker hanging by a piece of chain from its handles or seen a lighting fixture with a broken plug? This sort of equipment setup should make you nervous because it is not safe. In live sound, safety is often overlooked, sometimes through inexperience and sometimes through neglect and procrastination. Many of us have had gigs where all we wanted to do was get in, get the job done, and get out. But no matter what the mentality of the gig is, safety should always come first. Electrical guidelines are most commonly abused. Never perform a temporary electrical tie-in by yourself! In other words, opening and connecting inside an electrical panel. This is a job for a certified electrician and it is illegal to have it done by anybody else.

It is also incorrect to install an AC ground lift adapter and not connect the ground lug to the screw terminal centered between the plugs on the wall outlet. In the event of any fire, injury or death, you could be found responsible. Make a habit of running any snakes or cables over the top of doorways or exits instead of leaving them on the ground where people can trip over them. If the Fire Marshall makes a surprise inspection (and it sometimes happens) he may shut down your show until the problem is fixed.

Hanging loudspeakers (often called "flying" loudspeakers) should only be performed by a certified rigger. Riggers are specially trained in this field and always carry insurance in case of an accident. Only speakers manufactured with rated flying hardware can be flown safely. Never fly from handles!

It is commonplace to hang lighting equipment, but each fixture must be hung from a C-Clamp and should have a steel-rope safety chain. It is also a good idea to thoroughly inspect any lighting truss provided by the house before rigging your lights. If you are using a stepladder, never stand on the top step.

Lastly, always get help when lifting heavy cases or speakers.

Troubleshooting the Sound System

Hum and Buzz

One of the most common problems in PA systems is Hum & Buzz. The number one cause for this is ground loops.

Ground loops are most often caused by plugging the AC power for different pieces of equipment into different AC power circuits. For example, you may plug your mixer into a circuit on stage left and plug a power amp into a circuit on stage right. To eliminate this potential ground loop, you should plug all your equipment into one circuit. Or, if you feel that one 20-amp circuit is not sufficient to run all of your equipment, you should use multiple circuits from the same main circuit-breaker panel.

Another commonly used solution to the ground loop problem is to use a ground lift adapter on the AC plug. In some cases, this method effectively breaks the ground loop. It also defeats the electrical safety ground of your equipment. This could be a potentially fatal mistake! Under NO circumstances should the safety ground EVER be defeated. Instead, eliminate the ground loop by trying a different circuit, or even better, plug all your equipment into the same circuit or multiple circuits in the same circuit-breaker panel.

Hum and Buzz in audio is a very common problem. There are a number of causes, and solutions can sometimes be very elusive. Another possible cause of Hum and Buzz could be defective or poor quality cables. Remember, high quality components are only as good as the cables that connect them. If at all possible, avoid using cable adapters to accomplish connections. Instead use a more reliable custom-made cable.

Feedback Control

Anyone who has dealt with stage monitors will tell you it is a constant battle to obtain adequate volume levels without causing feedback. When you place a microphone near a loudspeaker that is ultimately fed by that microphone, you are going to get feedback as soon as the speaker output reaches unity gain. In order to get the most out of your stage monitor system before feedback, here are two common-sense tips, and two not-so-common tips.

• **Step 1: Always use directional microphones**. Cardioid or hypercardioid mics are the best choice. Notice that many of these mics have vents at the rear of the mic head or possibly in the mic handle. These vents give the mic its directional characteristics. Avoid covering these vents. Doing so will cause the mic to lose its directivity and its ability to reject feedback.

• **Step 2: Apply equalization if needed.** It is possible to use channel EQ to reduce feedback, but it is generally better to apply EQ at the input to the power amp. A 1/3 octave graphic EQ is most commonly used to reduce feedback in monitor systems. In some cases, a parametric EQ, or notch filter, is used in conjunction with a graphic EQ. This combination of graphic and parametric EQs is actually very effective. Stand-alone units are available for this purpose.

Other lesser known remedies for feedback include polarity reversal and time delay. Reversing the polarity can reduce feedback because instead of having the direct and reinforced sound waves adding together and thereby exceeding the threshold of feedback, they subtract from one another. Sometimes this is called reversing the phase. Reversing the phase or polarity simply means exchanging the two conductors in the audio signal line. This can be done by either switching the conductors at the speaker input or by switching the conductors of the balanced input on the microphone line by using a phase reversal adapter.

Time delay is a theoretically complex subject, but is easily applied. Introduce 20 to 30 milliseconds of signal delay into the system before the amplifier and before any graphic or parametric EQ is applied by using a simple digital delay unit. This trick will usually allow performers, especially vocalists, to hear themselves much better with less overall level. There is then less of a feedback problem because less gain is required.

In review, control feedback in stage monitors by:

• Use directional microphones, and
• If possible, use a combination of graphic EQ and a parametric or notch filter EQ together in a single unit.
• Apply alternative tricks used by the pros including polarity reversal and a 20 to 30 millisecond time delay.

Equipment Backup

Every DJ that relies upon his or her own sound system for his or her performance should be prepared for emergencies by keeping a few key system components around as backup equipment. Of course if you have lots of money to spare, you could just keep two of everything.

There are certain system components that are more likely to fail than others. Microphones and mic cables probably take more physical abuse than any other part of the sound system. Pay close attention to your mics at sound check and replace them with a spare if needed. Also be sure to keep more than one spare mic cable around.

Speaker cones and drivers are always at risk. Keeping a replacement speaker on hand is a very good idea. One way to save expensive speaker re-coning costs or outright speaker replacement is to use speakers with what are known as "field-replaceable baskets." It costs about half as much to replace the entire speaker cone and voice coil of this type of speaker and it can be done in about 15 minutes right on the job.

Remember, try to keep a spare for any component you feel is likely to ruin a show if it goes bad. Modern electronics are becoming more reliable, but you can never be too prepared for an important show.

Audio Tech Tips

The Audio Toolbox

Whether you are a DJ or a seasoned audio professional, you know that in live sound problems occur in many ways, usually when you don't expect them, and always when you don't need them. To help remedy problems, a thoroughly stocked audio tool box is a must.

Items in a good audio toolbox range from the most basic of tools to custom-made adapter cables and even to some sophisticated home-made gadgets. Never go to a gig without your tool kit.

Let's start with the basics. To save space, use a 4-in-1 screwdriver that includes a Phillips-head and a flat-head in two different sizes. A 6 or 8-inch crescent wrench, vise-grip and needle-nose pliers, wire-strippers, diagonal wire-cutters, and a set of metric and standard size Allan wrenches lay a good foundation of tools. Other basics are jewelers' screwdrivers, a mini-mag flashlight, and black electrical tape.

A simple multi-meter and an AC circuit tester are useful for determining the condition of an AC outlet. Proper voltage between 110 and 125 volts and no open grounds or reversed hot/neutral wires are essential for the safe operation of your equipment.

No field technician should be without a soldering iron and assorted supplies. A 60-watt soldering iron is a good choice as are, rosin-core electrical solder, and a sponge for keeping your solder-tip clean.

Always have plenty of spare adapters. Professional kits contain custom-made cable adapters that allow virtually any combination of connections to be made; they only use high quality cable and connectors. Double-check all solder-joints to make sure adapters are reliable and noise-free. Some of the most commonly used combinations include: ¼-inch phone plugs to male or female XLRs, "turnarounds" such as male to male XLRs or female to female XLRs, and RCA to male XLR for CD and cassette players. Some specialty adapters and gadgets include phase reversals, "pin 1 lifts" used to break ground loops, 15dB attenuation pads, and RF filters for microphone inputs. Be sure to have extra mic and speaker wire in your arsenal.

How to Solder

Soldering is a must-have skill for a DJ. It is also a skill that must be taught correctly and developed through practice.

Other than basic tools, four pieces of equipment will get the job done.

• Soldering audio cables and connectors requires a 50-to-60 watt soldering iron. Use of a higher wattage risks overheating the cable's insulation.

• Use only rosin-core solder for electronic work. Never use acid-core solder as this may corrode your connector.

• A wet sponge or rag is necessary for cleaning the tip of the soldering iron before and after each use.

• A small portable vise is very useful for holding the connector.

Make sure the area to be soldered is clean of any grease, dirt, or corrosion. Always use the soldering iron to heat the parts being soldered and never use it to melt the solder directly. A good solder joint is shiny and smooth in appearance when done correctly. When letting the solder joint set, it is necessary to keep it from moving around, otherwise a bad solder joint (known as a "cold" solder joint) which is characterized by a dull and rough finish, will result. Cold solder joints can be fixed by re-heating the joint and adding a small amount of new solder to the original spot.

When joining a wire to a connector, strip the wire back approximately ¼ inch and twist the strands together tightly. "Tin" the wire by coating it with solder. Apply a small amount of solder to the tip of the iron. This helps conduct heat to the connector, but is not the solder that will make up the joint. Now coat the mounting terminal with the solder that will form the joint. Hold the wire on the mounting terminal and heat the joint just enough to melt the solder on the connector and the wire. Then quickly remove the heat and hold steady to avoid a cold solder joint.

Chapter Notes

Operations

This chapter offers you basic practical tips for operating your business. Included are sample forms and contracts that you can adapt for your business. Be sure to visit the Web site where you will find more operations procedures. For more details see Chapter 9, *The Web Site.*

Event Planning Sheet

Please return this form no later that 2 weeks before your event.

Event contact:_____

Telephone:_____

Start time of event:_____ End time of event:_____

Location:_____

Event directions:

_____
_____
_____
_____

Is the reception on the first floor? _____ Is there an elevator? _____

Please list special announcements here:

_____
_____
_____
_____

Are there any activities or family traditions that you would like performed?

_____
_____
_____
_____

What concerns are important to you regarding your DJ and how he/she
coordinates your event?

_____
_____
_____
_____

Number of people attending your event?_____

Age of group_____

Special provisions and Additional Services Requested

_____

_____

_____

_____

_____

How much do you want the DJ to talk? (circle one)
Background Music/Simple Announcements/Crowd Participation

Will you be serving a meal?_____
When?_____

When is the best time to get in touch with you?_____
Telephone number:_____

E-mail address:_____

Music Request Sheet

Please return this form to us no later than 2 weeks before your event.

1._____	16._____
2._____	17._____
3._____	18._____
4._____	19._____
5._____	20._____
6._____	21._____
7._____	22._____
8._____	23._____
9._____	24._____
10._____	25._____
11._____	26._____
12._____	27._____
13._____	28._____
14._____	29._____
15._____	30._____

Radio stations you listen to:

_____

_____

_____

Songs that should *not* be played:

1._____ 5._____

2._____ 6._____

3._____ 7._____

4._____ 8._____

Sample Contract

AGREEMENT made this _____ day of _____, 20__, by and between _____, hereinafter referred to as the Purchaser, and *Your* DJ Service, hereinafter referred to as the DJ Service.

WITNESS NOW THEREFORE, in consideration of the promises and the agreements herein contained and intending to be legally bound hereby, the Parties do agree as follows:

1. The Purchaser hereby engages the DJ to provide a DJ Service. The service to be performed at Event Location:

Event Description:

_____

_____

_____

Address:

_____

_____

_____

_____

_____ Zip:_____

Telephone:_____

2. DJ Service hereby agrees to provide a DJ Service for the Purchaser at the above-mentioned location.

3. DJ Service shall consist primarily of providing musical entertainment by means of a recorded music format.

4. DJ Service hereby agrees to render his professional services and is at all times to have complete control of the musical program. This in absence of prearranged program requests received by Purchaser within deadline established by DJ Service.

5. The Parties hereby agree that the DJ Service shall be provided and accepted on the following date(s) and time(s) of the engagement:

Date(s): _____

Start Time(s): _____AM/PM

Finish Time(s): _____AM/PM

(4 hours minimum)

6. The Purchaser in consideration of the DJ Service to be rendered by the DJ, and the mutual promises contained herein, hereby agrees to pay to the DJ the following:

• A non-refundable reservation fee of $_____, is required to secure the services of DJ Service for the engagement. This amount shall be applied toward the Performance Fee.

• The Performance Fee is $_____ for the time frame outlined above.

• Services requested that exceed the 4-hour minimum time frame will be charged at the rate of $_____ per hour, payable the day of the engagement. It may not always be possible to provide additional performance time. However, when feasible, requests for extended playing time will be accommodated.

Additional Terms and Conditions

The agreement of the DJ to perform is subject to proven detention by accidents, riots, strikes, epidemics, acts of God, or any other legitimate conditions beyond their control. If such circumstances arise, all reasonable efforts will be made by DJ Service to find replacement entertainment at the agreed upon fees. Should DJ Service be unable to procure a replacement, Purchaser shall receive a full refund. Purchaser agrees that in all circumstances, DJ Service liability shall be exclusively limited to an amount equal to the performance fee and that DJ Service shall not be liable for indirect or consequential damages arising from any breach of contract.

All deposits are nonrefundable if cancelled by purchaser within 30 days prior to the event date. If DJ cancels the engagement, a full refund to Purchaser will be made.

The purchaser and DJ agree that this contract is not subject to cancellation unless both parties have agreed to such cancellation in writing. In the event the Purchaser breaches the contract, he or she shall pay the DJ the amount set forth above as "Wage agreed upon" as liquidated damages, 6% interest thereon, plus a reasonable attorney's fee.

In the event of non-payment, DJ Service retains the right to attempt collection through the courts. Purchaser will be held responsible for all court fees, legal fees, and collection costs incurred by DJ Service. Purchaser shall be charged $25 for each bounced check plus a $10 service charge for each collection notice.

No performance on the engagement shall be recorded, reproduced, or transmitted from the place of performance, in any manner, or any means whatsoever, in the absence of a specific written agreement with DJ Service relating to and permitting such recording, reproduction, or transmission. Pictures and videotape of the event are permitted for the private use of the contracting party only.

It is hereby further agreed; that the Purchaser shall be held liable for any injury or damages to the DJ, or property of the DJ, while on the premises of said engagement, if damage is caused by Purchaser or guest, members of his organization, engagement invitees, employees, or any other party in attendance, whether invited or not.

It is understood that if this is a "Rain or Shine" event, DJ Services compensation is in no way affected by inclement weather. For outdoor performances, Purchaser shall provide overhead shelter for setup area. See provision (*) below. The DJ reserves the right, in good faith, to stop or cancel the performance should the weather pose a potential danger to him, the equipment, or audience. Every effort will be made to continue the performance. However, safety is paramount in all decisions. The DJ's compensation will not be affected by such cancellation.

In the event of circumstances deemed to present a threat or implied threat of injury or harm to DJ Service staff or any equipment in DJ Service possession, DJ Service reserves the right to cease performance. If the Purchaser is able to resolve the threatening situation in a reasonable amount of time (maximum of 30 minutes), DJ Service shall resume performance in accordance with the original terms of this agreement. Purchaser shall be responsible for payment in full, regardless of whether the situation is resolved or whether DJ Service resumes performance. In order to prevent equipment damage or liability arising from accidental injury to any individual attending this performance, DJ Service reserves the right to deny any guest access to the sound system, music recordings, or other equipment.

* Purchaser shall provide DJ Service with safe and appropriate working conditions. This includes a 6-foot by 6-foot area for setup, space for setting up speakers and lighting stands. DJ Service requires a minimum of one 15-20-amp circuit outlet from a reliable power source within 50 feet (along the wall) of the set-up area. This circuit must be free of all other connected loads. Any delay in the performance or damage to DJ's equipment due to improper power is the responsibility of the purchaser. Two circuits are preferred, where possible. Additional outlets on separate circuits for lighting (if contracted for) are required. Purchaser shall provide crowd control if warranted; and furnish directions to place of engagement. Purchaser is responsible for paying any charges imposed by the venue. These charges may include, but are not limited to, parking, use of electric power, and fire marshal if necessary .

The Purchaser shall at all times have complete control, direction, and supervision of the performance of DJ Service at this engagement, and Purchaser expressly reserves the right to control the manner, means and details of the performance of the services of DJ Service. A written event/music planner or music request list must be received from the Purchaser and forwarded to DJ Service at least two weeks prior to the date of the engagement in order to be included in DJ Service programming guidelines. With or without the aid of an event/music planner or music request list, DJ Service shall attempt to play Purchaser's and Purchaser's guests' music requests; however, shall not be held responsible if certain selections are unavailable. DJ Service will make an extra effort to have music requests available if they are received in writing at least two weeks prior to the engagement. Purchaser certifies that all entertainment permits for event are up to date and agrees to show DJ Service on demand copies thereof.

This agreement guarantees that DJ Service will be ready to perform at the start time of the engagement. No guarantee is made as to DJ Service time of arrival; however, DJ Service requests that they be permitted _____ minutes before the engagement and _____ minutes after the engagement for setup and takedown. DJ Service also requests ramp or elevator access between the parking/service entrance and the setup area. If the event requires setup or takedown in less time, or if equipment must be carried up stairs or lifted onto a stage to reach the setup area, additional labor will be charged at a flat rate of $50. If Purchaser or event requires DJ Service to complete setup more than one hour before the start time, or to postpone takedown more than hour after the end time indicated, the additional time will be charged at the rate of $50 per half-hour.

Events requiring travel outside of our primary service area will be charged at $0.50 per mile in excess of 30 miles. Engagements in excess of 250 miles will require accommodations be made for an overnight stay in a local hotel/motel for DJ Service.

By executing this contract as Purchaser, the person executing said contract, either individually, or as an agent or representative, represents and warrants that he or she is eighteen (18) years of age, and further, if executing said contract as agent or representative, that he or she has the authority to enter into this agreement and should he or she not have such authority, he or she personally accepts and assumes full responsibility and liability under the terms of this contract.

All attached riders are an integral part of this contract. This contract will supersede any other contract. If any part of this contract is illegal or unenforceable, the remaining provisions of this contract will remain valid and enforceable to both parties. This contract contains the entire agreement between the parties and no statement, promises, or inducements made by any party hereto, or agent or representative or either party hereto, which are not contained in this written contract, shall be valid or binding. This contract shall not be enlarged, modified, or altered except in writing by both parties and endorsed hereon.

Purchaser agrees to defend, indemnify, assume liability for and hold DJ Service harmless from any claims, damages, losses, and expenses by or to any person, regardless of the basis, which pertain directly or indirectly to DJ Service performance. In the event that a civil action arises in an effort to enforce any provision of this agreement, the losing party shall pay the attorney's fee and court costs of the prevailing party. Purchaser may not transfer this contract to another party without the prior written consent of DJ Service.

This agreement is not binding until signed by both Purchaser and DJ Service, and each party has received a copy of it. Any changes must be written and signed by both the Purchaser and DJ Service. Oral agreements are non-binding. If any clause in this agreement is found to be illegal, the rest of the agreement shall remain in force.

DJ Service may elect not to exercise their rights as specified in this agreement. By doing so, DJ Service does not waive their right to exercise those options at a future date.

The laws of the State of _____ shall govern this agreement. In the event of lawsuit involving or relating to this agreement, Purchaser agrees that venue will be in _____ County.

THE PARTIES hereto promise to abide by the terms of this agreement and intend to be legally bound thereby.

Purchaser:

_____
Signature

_____

Printed Name _____
Street Address: _____

_____
Daytime Phone: _____
Evening Phone: _____

DJ Service:

_____

Customer Follow-up Survey Form

Please check your response:

1. How would you rate our pre-event planning services?

      Good ____ Average____ Poor____

2. Did we set-up in a timely manner?

      Good ____ Average____ Poor____

3. Did we meet your expectations during your event?

      Good ____ Average____ Poor____

4. What can we do to improve our services?

_____

_____

_____

_____

_____

_____

_____

_____

5. May we use your name and contact information as a reference?

Yes ____ No____

If yes, please provide your contact information:

Name: _____

Address: _____

_____

                Zip:_____

Telephone:_____

Email:_____

Signed:_____

Printed Name:_____

THANK YOU!

Financing Your DJ Service

This chapter offers you a quick overview of some of the sources where you might find to help finance your DJ service. From partners, family, friends, government loan programs, to credit cards, this chapter offers strategies to help you get the start-up capital you will need.

Money Sources

Where are you going to get the money to start your DJ service? Will you:

• Provide the money yourself from savings or existing equity?
• Take a loan from a bank or the government?
• Get a loan from friends and family?
• Provide an equity stake in your business to business partners?
• Credit cards?

There are many ways to approach the financing of your venture. I will discuss a few of them here. Keep in mind that you can use a combination of these when exploring the financing of your business.

You Have The Money

By far, the easiest way to obtain money to start your business is to provide it yourself. You might have savings that you can dip into, or you may have property with equity that you can use to borrow against. You may want to consider providing some of your savings and the rest in a loan. For example, you could provide half your start-up capital from your savings and the other half from a property equity line.

Property equity lines are relatively easy to get these days. Basically, these are secured loans that are based on the value of your property. For example, if you paid $100,000 for your house and the appraised value is $125,000, you could borrow $25,000, which is the equity that you have built in the property over time. The bank protects itself by securing the loan. This means that if you do not pay back the loan, the bank can foreclose on your property and force the sale of the property to pay back the loan.

The Bank Has The Money

The reality is that most banks will not loan you money unless you have collateral that they can use to secure a loan. You can't blame them. They are in business too, and must protect their interests. You can dress up in your Sunday suit and take your spit-polished business plan into a meeting and try to convince a banker to loan you all the money to start your venture. However, be ready for rejection.

Banks generally do not make loans for DJ services because there is no collateral stake that they can make. For example if loans are not repaid, they know that the value of used equipment, goes down fast. So, if they had loaned you money based on the new market price, they would be in the hole if they had to sell the assets to pay for delinquent loans.

The Government Has The Money

The United States Small Business Administration (SBA) might invest in your idea by providing you with a loan. However, they generally provide business planning assistance through associations like their Small Business Development Centers and The Service Corps of Retired Executives (SCORE). The government has grant money available; however, qualification parameters are constantly changing. To get an idea of what is available go to the Small Business Administrations Internet Web site at *www.sba.gov.*

*Download the Ebook, **The Government Loan Resource Guide**, at the Web site.*

Family and Friends Have The Money

Family and friends can be a good source for funds. As long as you treat these sources with respect and show them your plans, you may find an early supporter in your quest for start-up capital. Keep all business relationships professional, even if family and friends are involved.

Personal relationships can be destroyed if there is no attention paid to the business side of the relationship. If someone loans you money, sign a note of promise to pay, with the specific terms of repayment set fourth in the note. This will make for a better relationship overall because you will be showing your friend and/or family member that you are a responsible business person.

Partners

Many people form partnerships to assist in the financing of a business and to help share and limit risk. Working partners generally have a say in how the business is run; silent partners do not. There are many ways to set up partnerships. For example, in order to maintain decision control of your company, you can elect to have silent partners, whereby they will be provided an equal share of the ownership of the business in exchange for their investment.

Credit Cards

In today's credit-happy society, banks are eager to provide credit cards to almost anybody. Once you establish good credit through the credit bureaus, the banks will be sending you unsolicited applications with lines of credit and generous repayment interest rate terms. Credit cards are basically unsecured lines of credit, meaning that there is no collateral needed to obtain them. Interest rates can be higher than more conventional loans; however, they can help with some of your start-up expenses when establishing your business. As with any loan, be sure to include these loan expenses as part of your start-up expense.

Your Plan of Attack

Keep in mind that financing your business is going to be one of the most difficult aspects of starting up. It is going to demand that you establish your credibility and integrity with people. Creativity can be your key to success in regard to how you choose to approach loans from banks, government, friends, and partners.

Your business plan is your critical success tool. Your plan will tell prospective investors what your concept is and what you are all about. Don't be shy. Show your plan with pride. When asked a specific question, say, "...let's see what page that is on...", and turn to the specific page in your business plan. Once you do this, the demeanor of your prospect will change immediately.

Establish your credibility by sharing with your prospect your professional background and why you are convinced your business concept will work. Be enthusiastic and knowledgeable about your goals.

Constructive Criticism

Listen and adapt. Bankers, friends, and family might offer suggestions about how you can improve your pitch for a loan. If they do, don't get defensive. Instead adapt your business plan and loan pitch to deal with their objections. The main element in your proposal is personal selling. You are selling yourself and your ideas. In order to successfully close the sale, you will need to deal with all of the prospects objections.

Obtaining funds for your DJ service can be a daunting task. It can be a time-consuming and sometimes frustrating project. However, with persistence and organization you will prevail.

Remember, never quit!

Chapter Notes

The Web Site

www.bizventures.com/dj

This chapter explains some of the products and services that you will find at the Web site, which accompanies this book. Many of the software programs are available as demos and some are free. Be sure to return your registration card so that you will be able to access the site. Also, you will find an errata section at the site where you will find, or post typos and specific information about pages in this book

Software

JustDoIt! Project Management Software

JustDoIt! is a project management tool designed to keep your project on track. What is a project?

A project is starting a DJ service. Simply load a sample project into the program and then edit. We highly recommend that you use this program from the very start of your endeavors because it will help budgeting and keep you on track. The manual for this program is in a file called just-doit.pdf, for Adobe Acrobat Reader. Once installed, study the example project files to see how simple it is to create your own project(s).

Employee Shift Scheduling Software

If you are running a multi-shift employee operation, then Scheduling Employees for Windows is a must! This award winning software program is a cinch to learn and will pay big dividends. This program is fantastic!

Safety Advisor Software

OSHA Software Application Programs

Government regulations play a key role in your activities as a DJ service operator. We have assembled some expert systems that you can be use to establish sections of your operations manual. Simply install the software and answers the questions. Policies will be generated for you automatically.

Safety Pays

Safety Pays is a tool developed by the Occupational Safety and Health Administration (OSHA) to assist employers in assessing the impact of occupational injuries and illnesses on their profitability. It uses a company's profit margin, the average costs of an injury or illness, and an indirect cost multiplier to project the amount of sales a company would need to generate in order to cover those costs.

Fire Safety

The Fire Safety Advisor program provides interactive expert help. It addresses OSHA's general industry standards for fire safety and emergency evacuation, and for fire fighting, fire suppression, and fire detection systems and equipment. Once installed on your PC, it asks you about office and business policies and practices. It asks follow-up questions based on your answers to prepare the guidance and write the customized plans you need.

Hazard Awareness

The Hazard Awareness Program is powerful, interactive, expert software to identify hazards in general industry workplaces. It will ask you about your workplace, and ask follow-up questions based on your answers. It will write you a customized report about possible hazards and related OSHA rules.

Safety and Health

This Expert Advisor will help you review and evaluate key aspects of your safety and health program, if you have one. If you do not have one, it could help you think about elements of a good program. It is straight-forward and very easy to use.

Occupational Safety and Health Administration (OSHA)

Here you will find various documents that will help you with OSHA inspections and assist with job-hazard analysis procedures that will become part of your operations manual.

• OSHA inspections.
• OSHA handbook for small business.
• Job hazard analysis.
• What to expect during OSHA's visit.

Posters

Here you will find government informational posters that you will be required to post in your establishment.

• Job safety poster.
• Equal opportunity poster.
• Equal opportunity poster in Spanish.
• Employee polygraph protection act poster.
• Employee family medical leave act poster.
• Employee family medical leave act poster in Spanish.

Bonus
Download the Microsoft Word and Excel spreadsheets that go with the business plan in Chapter 5, The Business Plan. Edit them and you will have your business plan ready to go!

Also, Download the forms and sample contract found in Chapter 7, Operations.

Ebooks

We have put together a series of electronic books that you can download. This is only a partial listing, so be sure to check the site for the latest additions.

- How to Get a Trademark.
- How to Get a Patent.
- The Government Loan Resource Guide.

CD-ROM

We have a CD-ROM available for purchase with the contents of the Web site. This way you can have all the contents at your fingertips for quick access. See the registration form at the back of the book for details about how to order.

The optional CD-ROM, contains the same information and software that you will find at the Web site. We have made it available for purchase for those of you who want to have the information available first hand.

Appendix

Knowledge

This is the appendix. Here you will find a supplemental information, contact list, and bibliography.

Associations, Referral Services and Trade Magazines

American Disc Jockey Association
www.adja.org

Canadian Online Disc Jockey Association
www.codja.com

Mobile Entertainers Alliance
www.usmea.org

N.A.M.E. - The National Association of Mobile Entertainers
www.djkj.com

ProDJ.com
www.prodj.com

Untited States Online Disc Jockey Association
www.usodja.com

Disc Jockey 1-800
www.800dj.com

Disc Jockey Referral Network
http://djnet.com

Trade Magazines

DJ Times
www.djtimes.com

Extreme Groove
www.extremegroove.com

Mobile Beat
www.mobilebeat.com

Remix
www.remixmag.com

Government

U.S. Small Business Administration
www.sba.gov
www.business.gov

U.S. Internal Revenue Service
www.irs.gov

U.S. Federal Trade Commission
www.ftc.gov

U.S. Department of Labor
www.dol.gov

Equipment and Music Program Material

Abracadabra
www.thedjproshop.com

Electronic Bargins
www.electronicbargins.com

Musician's Friend
www.musiciansfriend.com

Sam Ash
www.samash.com

Six Star DJ
www.sixstardj.com

Sweetwater Sound
www.sweetwater.com

The Source for Music
www.thesourceformusic.com

Promo Only
www.promoonly.com

Bibliography

Business Buyer's Handbook, by Jim Calkins. Published by Oak Tree Publishing, Claremont, California.

Fundamentals of Production/Operations Management, by Harold E. Fearon. Published by West Publishing Company, Los Angeles, California.

Principles of Accounting, by Melvin Morgenstein. Published by HBJ Media Systems Corporation, New York, New York.

Marketing, by Carl McDaniel, Jr. Published by Harper & Row, New York, New York.

Marketing Management: Strategy and Cases, by Douglas J. Dalrymple. Published by John Wiley & Sons, New York, New York.

Music, Speech, High Fidelity, by William J. Strong and George R. Plitnik, Second edition. Published by Soundprint.

Music, Money and Success, by Jeffrey and Todd Brabec, Second edition. Published by Schirmer Trade Books, New York, New York.

Modern Recording Techniques, by Robert E. Runstein. Published by Howard W. Sams & Company, New York, New York.

Home Recording for Musicians, by Craig Anderton. Published by Guitar Player Books.

The Recording Studio Handbook, by John M. Woram. Published by Sagamore Publishing Company, Plainview, New York.

Audio Cyclopedia, by Howard M. Tremaine. Published by Howard W. Sams & Company, New York, New York.

Multi-Track Recording, by Brent Hurtig. Published by, GPI Publications, Cupertino, California.

Index

Notes

Notes

Notes

Notes

Notes

About the Author

Dan Titus was raised in Southern California. He is a musician, producer and writer. Dan graduated in 1987 from California State University Long Beach with a Bachelor of Science in Marketing. He has been involved in multimedia business consulting for the past several years and is president of Venture Marketing, a business media publishing firm. When not researching and consulting, Dan enjoys writing songs and spending time with his family.

Product Registration Form

Yes! I want my free Web site access...

Name_____

Company_____

Address_____

City_____State_____ Zip_____

Country_____

Telephone_____

Web site_____

Email_____

(Important: We will email you your Web site access code)

Where did you purchase your book?

_____

Age_____ Male_____ Female____

CD-ROM Order

Please send me *The DJ Cookbook Business Start-up Guide CD-ROM* for only $24.95 plus $5.00 shipping and handling to the address above.

___ I have enclosed a check.

___ I wish to pay via credit card:

___ American Express ___ Master Card ___Visa

Card Holders Name_____

Credit Card Number_____

Expiration Date_____

Card Holders Signature_____

Mail This Completed Form To:

Venture Marketing, Inc.

Box 151

Chino Hills CA 91709

- Cut along the dotted line and mail this form -

Never Quit.